The Book of
Flower Spells

The Book of
Flower Spells

CHERALYN DARCEY

ROCKPOOL

For my beautiful Flowerchild,
Maddison

Each separate flower has a magic all its own.
Myr

A Rockpool book
PO Box 252
Summer Hill
NSW 2130
Australia

rockpoolpublishing.com
Follow us! **f** ⓘ rockpoolpublishing
Tag your images with #rockpoolpublishing

ISBN 978-1-925682-25-0
A catalogue record for this book is available from the National Library of Australia.

First published in 2018
Copyright Text © Cheralyn Darcey 2018
Copyright Design © Rockpool Publishing 2018

Cover design by Richard Crookes
Internal design and typesetting by Jessica Le, Rockpool Publishing

Printed and bound in China

10 9 8 7 6 5

The information presented in this book is intended for general inquiry, research and informational purposes only and should not be considered as a substitute or replacement for any trained medical advice, diagnosis, or treatment. Always consult a registered herbalist before taking or using any preparations suggested in this book.

Contents

Foreword..ix

Welcome, Blossom...xiii

How To Use This Book...xvii

SECTION ONE: What Is A Spell and How Does It Work? 1

SECTION TWO: A Collection of Flower Spells......................... 17

　　Relationships and Love.. 19

　　Happiness and Harmony 41

　　Success and Prosperity 63

　　Protection and Clearing.. 85

　　Health and Healing..107

　　Transition and Change..129

SECTION THREE: How to Create Your Own Spells 153

　　Flower Spell Journal 157

　　Flower Meanings..165

　　Glossary...171

　　Bibliography 175

　　Image Credits.. 177

Foreword

I spent my childhood picking wild fruits and herbs in garden centres or in the untouched lands near my home, for Mum to cook with. I was deeply heartbroken when I returned to this childhood home years later to find it mowed down by high-rise flats on cold concrete landscapes. The opportunity to connect to Earth and her gifts in modern times is often waved away as a childish fantasy or an outdated practice, yet the impact of this disconnect is creating huge problems in our environment and mental health. It is through books like the one you are holding that we can reconnect with the world around us. To those who wave away our connectedness with Earth as a fantasy, I offer you an alternative way to consider these practices.

Whatever you believe, if any working in this book appeals to you, for whatever reason, be curious about this longing. It will reveal two things: a personal, important value; and the core belief behind it. These are very deep-seated revelations to consider. What is it about the ritual's potential outcome you want? How would you know if you have achieved this? What will change if you achieve this? Why is it important to you? What previous attempts have you already made to attain this need? How far away are you from this intended result? What do you 'feel' about this outcome? What could that feeling mean? Questioning then listening to yourself is extremely important to develop self-awareness, an internal focus for change, and to set the intent for your work. Intent is the central part to any working. Each working in this book has a clear intent.

The next thing you will notice in each of this book's workings is the suggested ritual components. Take the time to learn what the key ingredients are in your chosen working, where they are from, their history, their traditional, symbolic and practical uses, and the safest way in which to use them. This understanding will not only help you take control of the working, but turn the information it provides into knowledge for further personal use. A famous chef once told me: 'If you really learn one recipe a month, cooking it several times, learning about each ingredient, within a year not only will you know twelve recipes by heart, but you will be able to combine that knowledge into creating many additional dishes.' This book contains recipes with practical ingredients information that you can continue to use beyond ritual craft.

The ritual itself contains carefully planned ingredients and ritualistic movements as sensory symbolism for your unconscious mind to understand your intent and react. Our brains are naturally wired to notice, decode and interpret symbols, even better than the confines of language. From a technical viewpoint, a ritual can be considered a form of intentional reprogramming for your mind to perceive a situation differently, notice appropriate opportunities, or behave in a suggested way. Here we begin to understand how ritual work may not directly affect the world around us and those within it, per se, but instead alter our internal world to be more aligned and receptive with what we want to attract. This internal shift will change what we project externally and therefore create a new way of being. True personal change can take time and patience, so focus on participating in the beautiful transformative experience of the working itself, not the eventual outcome.

Live in the moment and be present.

Listen to your Inner Self. **Learn** all you can. **Live** in the moment. **Love** yourself.

This is true magick.

— Pip Stoneham, *The Serenity Oracle*

Pip is a fellow pagan, magick creator, artist and oracle writer and a great friend who I am blessed to share space with. Her work as well as her enthusiasm and dedication for the Pagan community is a blessing and something the world needs more of – people with passion, sharing what they know, discovering and loving generously.

Welcome, Blossom

No matter what path we are on, what our beliefs are, what our background is, where we live or what we do, plants are our constant companions. Even in the busiest city, you will not need to go far to share space with a plant of some kind; you will not need to look far to experience their benefits. They decorate our lives, provide oxygen, food, shelter, tools, medicines and inspiration, both emotional and spiritual, through our interactions with them.

Welcome to a book of living magickally with flowers. My passion is teaching and sharing the things I love and I've long wanted to create a book that anyone can use, no matter what their level of experience. Before we even begin, though, I want to make sure that you understand flowers and how to respectfully use them to create real magick.

Flowers are the reproductive organs of a plant and, as such, they are emotional in nature. They attract pollinators in a variety of ways, including using their looks, fragrance and texture as well as their energy. Along with their physical attributes, this energy is how we can connect with flowers to share their magick. Flowers illicit an emotional response from us, which connects us directly to their energy and, in doing so, makes them more desirable. We will acquire, tend, protect and assist what pleases or seems to help us, and this ensures the flowers' continuance.

The term 'ethnobotany' further describes the relationship between people and plants and it is my life work. I have found ethnobotany fascinating as well as incredibly rewarding to understand – the never-ending layers of connections we share with plants and how we can both benefit when working with respect and care, in harmony.

To discover what the individual energy of each flower is, we look at the way it behaves, its appearance, the things it provides. Lavender, for example, produces a fragrance that is naturally calming and cleansing. The colour indicates restfulness, and even the soft texture of the leaves and flowers leads us to a certain understanding of the energy of this plant.

A large part of my research includes botanical history, folklore and magick. This research, along with my upbringing in a Pagan family, has resulted in me creating and accumulating a very large collection of spells, rituals and blessings, which I have always found great benefit from. I am so delighted to share some of this knowledge with you in this special collection of flower spells.

Because I am dedicated to ensuring that botanical knowledge and the language of nature is not lost, I have also written this book in a way that will assist you in understanding why each flower is included. Magick and the language of nature are not things you need to find; they are within you already, but you have simply forgotten how to access them. With this book I hope to help you remember.

I also have an immense passion for what my family lovingly calls 'Cheralyn's Magickal Botanical Facts', which focus on gardening, botanical history and botany. So, sprinkled throughout this book of flower spells are tips, ideas, fascinating facts and a little bit of mythical magick which, as anyone who has met me in person knows, I adore sharing, hearing about, and delighting in. I hope you do too.

I hope that you find something here in this little book of Flower Spells and Magick, which will support, guide and inspire you.

May Nature bless you always, but I hope that you, too, be the blessing that Nature needs!

Bunches of Blessings,

Cheralyn

How To Use This Book

It's never an easy task creating an instructional book to suit everyone. What I do want to do is put my collection of flower spells into the hands of everyone who is interested in the magickal ways one can work with flowers.

The more experienced in spellcrafting and casting, or those who have dedicated and defined paths in their own beliefs, may be able to skim the following basic instruction pages and dive into the spells, experimenting and exploring new paths which my work may open up, enhance or complement. Those who have a small amount, to no experience, in magickal work are cared for with information to safely set them on their way to creating and casting spells.

It is my suggestion that all of you at least read through the first section to familiarise yourself with the foundations of the Nature magick in this book. For those who are complete beginners, or have some experience, *Section One* will provide a good grounding in safe and best practice when creating and casting flower spells as well as explaining in detail each spell and how it works.

I have shared 60 spells that I have written over my life, all of which focus on flowers and their energies. They are arranged in smaller chapters by their use so that you can quickly find a spell that suits your needs. Make sure you observe the instructions I have given, or your own unique approach, each time you are creating and casting spells.

All the steps to using each spell are clearly explained and also provide a simple, everyday ingredients list and tools. I also share additional interesting and helpful tips with each spell to enrich your experience working with Nature and so you can get to know our flower friends a little bit more.

At the end of this collection is a very special journal, a place to keep your own spells. First I have provided a simple guide to writing your own magick and then a collection of beautiful pages that you may use to keep your flower spells together with mine.

What if you don't have fresh flowers?

As wonderful as it would be to access every flower on Earth no matter where you found yourself, the reality is you cannot. I have given you alternate flowers that hold similar energies and which you may be able to source easily. I would also encourage you to dry your own flowers when they are available and create or source essences, candles, incenses and other botanical treasures so you have a magickal apothecary to rely on.

What if you don't have flowers at all?

To further focus energy or to connect with flowers when don't you have access to them, imagery in the form of artwork, photos, your sketches or oracle cards can be used. I feel it is very important to see the flower to connect with its unique energy.

Caryphyll maximi, et pleniß. colore mixto, carneo qbusdam corniculis lacteis.

TAB. CXXII.

Melanth flore.
multiplici coeruleo

Melanthium
hispanicu
amplo flore.
dilute Viola
ceo

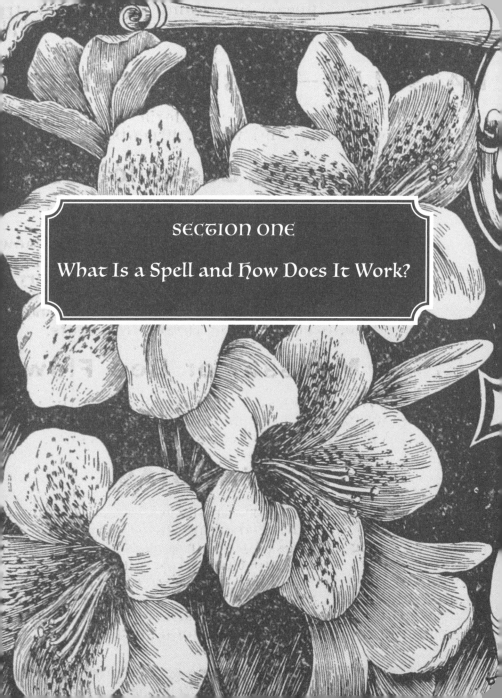

SECTION ONE

What Is a Spell and How Does It Work?

A spell is a combination of ingredients, tools, actions and focus, which come together energetically to create change. Timings (when you cast your spell) can also be observed to ensure added power. These timings can be Moon or astrological phases, seasonal times and also correspondences that connect with days of the week or hours of the day or night.

❧ TIMINGS

These are the times that you put spells together and cast them. They add an energetic boost to your spells by bringing alignment to what you are doing in the space you are creating the spell. I'm sharing simple timings here for you, but you can also explore deeper, seasonal timings – ones associated with traditional pagan celebrations and observances and ones that are unique to your area and people as well as being open to other peoples.

Moon Phases
» *Waxing:* new projects, beginnings, growth
» *Full:* empowerment, healing, attainment
» *Waning:* banishing, cleansing, letting go
» *New:* divination, revelations

Day of the Week

» *Monday:* home, family, dreams, emotions, female energies, gardens, medicine, psychic development, travel

» *Tuesday:* courage, strength, politics, conflict, lust, endurance, competition, surgical procedures, sports, masculine energies

» *Wednesday:* communication, divination, self-improvement, teaching, inspiration, study, learning

» *Thursday:* luck, finances, legal matters, desires, honour, accomplishments, prosperity, material gain

» *Friday:* friendship, pleasure, art, music, social activities, comfort, sensuality, romance

» *Saturday:* life, protection, self-discipline, freedom, wisdom, goals, reincarnation

» *Sunday:* spirituality, power, healing, individuality, hope, healing, professional success, business

Time of the Day

» *Dawn:* beginnings, awakening, cleansing, new ideas, change, love

» *Morning:* growth, home, gardening, finances, harmony, generosity

» *Midday:* health, willpower, physical energy, intellect

» *Afternoon:* communication, business, clarity

» *Dusk/Twilight:* reduction, change, receptiveness

» *Night:* pleasure, joy, socialising, gatherings, play

» *Midnight:* endings, release, recuperation

❦ INGREDIENTS

The ingredients you gather to create the spell will have correspondences to your intention. In a way, they illustrate what it is that you want to happen.

They will support the things you wish to happen because they have similar meanings and energies. These meanings and energies may also assist you in removing something. These correspondences are important because they also help us find substitute ingredients for our spells when what is prescribed is not available. I will give you my suggestions with each spell.

❦ TOOLS

Tools are additional items that you can use to help you create your spell. These are just a few examples of tools used in spellcrafting and casting:

» cloths to set your spell up on (usually in colours which align with the energy of the spell)
» wands and staffs to direct and enhance energies
» divination tools such as tarot and oracle cards, crystal balls, pendulums and runes to provide clarity
» drums and bells (musical instruments and music express your intentions)
» practical items such as glasses, cups, vases, bowls and cutting tools.

The way you put a spell together, the words you may recite, the things you actually do to cast your spell are the actions that bring it all together. These focus your intention, put you squarely in the

path of the outcome and strengthen the relationship between the energies of the ingredients and the tools you are using. The combination of all these things raise the energy for magick to happen.

❧ WHY WOULDN'T A SPELL WORK?

Not many things in life work all the time. External factors influence them; maybe they are not put together properly; sometimes it is just not meant to be. I'm sitting here writing my book for you on my laptop. I love my little computer, but it's rather clunky at times and has had its moments. It closes down for no apparent reason, loses files, can't be bothered accepting my Airdrops and decides I need to look at all the files with a certain keyword except the one I want. It appears to have a mind of its own.

You cannot change another person's free will and this is also why spells do not work at times. Perhaps the consequence of the spell will adversely affect another or counter their stronger will, which you might not even be aware of. Another reason a spell may not work is because other energies have greater strength at that moment or they may in fact be leading you to a better eventual outcome.

Spells work because the person creating and casting them fully believes in what they are doing and has a strong, focused intention with a good connection to the energies of their spell and the outcome. While perhaps changing things for personal benefit, the outcome is still generally in keeping with a good outcome for all involved without forcibly changing anyone's free will.

❧ HOW TO CREATE AND CAST A SPELL

When you are using the spells in this book, please ensure you do so safely – and by this I don't just mean keeping burning candles attended to. Working with energies to create magick requires you to take responsibility for what you are doing, for yourself and the world you live in. There are many ways you can do this, just as there are many ways of life and beliefs with their own rituals, which ensure safety and power in spellcasting.

Most safety measures include a way to protect yourself and those around you. A way to mark the beginning of the spell or opening the space comes next. There will be words, meditation, music, chants or actions, which will help you focus on the task at hand, and then there will be a way to release the energy, perhaps give thanks and to close the space.

This is a simple and safe way to cast a spell.

Protect and Open

Before you can begin it's important to establish protection from negative energies. There are various ways you can achieve this, but whatever way you use make sure you always protect yourself before casting. You may wish to use a smudging method, by burning sage or other plants, or by spraying the room with a smudging mist. You can also visualise or draw a circle around you and your spell with your finger in the air, then fill your circle with white light.

If you are aligned with certain deities, elementals or guides, you may wish to ask for their assistance in providing protection. A very simple and effective protection method is to light a white candle while visualising the light cleansing, clearing and protecting you.

Focus Intention

Sit or stand still for a long moment and imagine your outcome. Really see it in your mind and complete your picture with exact times, places and events. You may like, at this time before you cast your spell, to write down your intention and say it out loud to get yourself fully focused and your energy aligned with what it is you are about to create.

Cast Spell

In each of the flower spells I have shared with you, I have set out very specific steps to create your spell and I have explained why I've used these steps. In the final section, I've provided instruction on creating your own spells. Casting your spell is simply what you do to make the spell happen. While casting your spell, you must maintain your focus on your intention.

Release, Close and Ground

Once you have completed your spell, you will need to release the power you have raised in creating it. I will provide a way to release the spell for each spell I share with you, but you can also simply say: 'I release the power I have raised' or 'It is done' or by putting out your white candle if lit.

Grounding is the way you bring yourself back from your spellcasting time. Clapping you hands, ringing a bell or placing your bare feet or hands on the earth are all ways to ground yourself.

❦ COLOUR

You can use colour in cloth, candles, flowers, additional ingredients and other tools, to set your spell upon.

» *Red:* passion, power, strength, courage, renewal, health, motivation, self-esteem, confrontation, ambition, challenge, purchases

» *Pink:* healing, calming, emotions, harmony, compassion, self-love, romance, relaxation, new beginnings, partnerships

» *Orange:* opportunities, legal matters, obstacles, abundance, gain, power, happiness

» *Yellow:* friendship, returns, productivity, creativity, education, healing

» *Green:* wellness, new beginnings, marriage, home, planning, peace, harmony, birth, rebirth, fertility, affection, luck, change, creativity, socialising

» *Blue:* self-improvement, opportunity, charity, study, growth, travel, insight, patience, meditation, sports, religion, social standing, expansion, higher education, wisdom
» *Brown:* focus, lost items, grounding, harvest, security, generosity, endurance
» *Violet:* psychic growth, divination, spiritual development, self-improvement
» *Purple:* spirit, ambition, protection, healing, intuition, business, occultism
» *White:* protection, safety, transformation, enlightenment, connection to higher self, becoming more outgoing, relieving shyness, the cycle of life, freedom, health, initiation
» *Black:* divination, rebirth, material gain, discoveries, truth, sacrifice, protection, creation, death, karma, absorbing energies, binding, neutralising, debts, separation.

❧ CRYSTALS

The addition of whole pieces of crystal, tumble stones, balls and jewellery can add specific energies to your spells. Not all crystals are suitable for all types of spells – some are not safe when they come in contact with items you use for consumption, or topically.

You will need to check the properties of the crystals before you create your spells. A reliable, specialised crystal-usage resource is advisable. Below is a basic summary of crystals and their properties:

» *Agate:* courage, longevity, love, protection, healing, self-confidence
» *Agate, Black:* success, courage
» *Agate, Black and White:* physical protection
» *Agate, Blue Lace:* peace, consciousness, trust, self-expression
» *Agate, Green Moss:* healing, longevity, gardening, harmony, abundance
» *Amazonite:* creativity, unity, success, thought process

- » *Amber:* protection, luck, health, calming, humour, spell breaker, manifestation
- » *Amethyst:* peace, love, protection, courage, happiness, psychic protection
- » *Apache Tear:* protection from negative energies, grief, danger, forgiveness
- » *Apatite:* control, communication, coordination
- » *Aquamarine:* calm, strength, control, fears, tension relief, thought processes
- » *Aventurine:* independence, money, career, sight, intellect, sport, leadership
- » *Azurite:* divination, healing, illusions, communication, psychic development
- » *Bloodstone:* healing, business, strength, power, legal matters, obstacles
- » *Calcite:* purification, money, energy, spirituality, happiness
- » *Carnelian:* courage, sexual energy, fear, sorrow release, action, motivation
- » *Chalcedony:* emotions, honesty, optimism
- » *Chrysocolla:* creativity, female energies, communication, wisdom
- » *Citrine:* detox, abundance, regeneration, cleansing, clarity, initiative
- » *Dioptase:* love attracter, prosperity, health, relaxation
- » *Emerald:* wealth, protection, intellect, artistic talent, tranquility, memory
- » *Epidote:* emotional healing, spirituality
- » *Fluorite:* study, intellect, comprehension, balance, concentration
- » *Garnet:* protection, strength, movement, confidence, devotion
- » *Gold:* power, success, healing, purification, honour, masculine energy
- » *Hematite:* divination, common sense, grounding, reasoning, relationships
- » *Herkimer Diamond:* tension-soothing, sleep, rest, power-booster
- » *Iolite:* soul connection, visions, discord release
- » *Jade:* justice, wisdom, courage, modesty, charity, dreams, harmony
- » *Jasper:* healing, health, beauty, nurturing, travel
- » *Jet:* finances, anti-nightmares, divination, health, luck, calms fears
- » *Kunzite:* addiction, maturity, security, divinity

- » *Kyanite:* dreams, creativity, vocalisation, clarity, serenity, channelling
- » *Labradorite:* destiny, elements
- » *Lapis Lazuli:* love, fidelity, joy, healing, psychic development, inner truth
- » *Larimar:* confidence, depression, serenity, energy balance
- » *Malachite:* money, sleep, travel, protection, business
- » *Moldavite:* changes, transformation, life purpose
- » *Moonstone:* youth, habits, divination, love, protection, friends
- » *Obsidian:* grounding, production, peace, divination
- » *Onyx:* stress, grief, marriage, anti-nightmares, self-control
- » *Opal:* beauty, luck, power, money, astral projection
- » *Pearl:* faith, integrity, innocence, sincerity, luck, money, love
- » *Peridot:* wealth, stress, fear, guilt, personal growth, health
- » *Prehnite:* chakras, relationships
- » *Pyrite:* memory, focus, divination, luck
- » *Quartz, Clear:* protection, healing, power, psychic power
- » *Quartz, Rose:* love, peace, happiness, companionship
- » *Quartz, Smokey:* depression, negativity, tension, purification
- » *Rhodochrosite:* new love, peace, energy, mental powers, trauma-healing
- » *Ruby:* wealth, mental balance, joy, power, contentment, intuition
- » *Sapphire:* meditation, protection, power, love, money, wisdom, hope
- » *Sardonyx:* progression, finances, self-protection
- » *Selenite:* decisions, reconciliation, flexibility, clarity
- » *Silver:* stress, travel, invocation, dreams, peace, protection, energy
- » *Sodalite:* wisdom, prophetic dreams, dissipates confusion
- » *Sugilite:* physical healing, heart, wisdom, spirituality
- » *Sunstone:* sexual healing, energy, protection, health
- » *Tanzanite:* magick, insight, awareness

- » *Tiger's Eye:* courage, money, protection, divination, energy, luck
- » *Topaz:* love, money, sleep, prosperity, commitment, calm
- » *Tourmaline:* friendship, business, health, astral projection
- » *Tourmaline, Black:* grounding, protection,
- » *Tourmaline, Blue:* peace, stress relief, clear speech
- » *Tourmaline, Green:* success, creativity, goals, connection with nature
- » *Tourmaline, Pink:* friendship, love, creativity
- » *Tourmaline, Red:* projection, courage, energy
- » *Turquoise:* protection, communication, socialising, health, creative solutions

❧ FLOWERS FOR SPELLS

In this book, I will be focusing on getting you to experience magick as easily as possible with everyday items. I will also share with you substitutions for any items that may be a little hard to obtain, especially flowers that may be out of season.

Tools and magickal ingredients can be obtained from bricks-and-mortar stores and online, but always be guided by your feelings when making purchases from these sellers. Make sure you feel comfortable and positive about these businesses because their energies will transfer. Make sure that anything that comes into your space to use for spell work has no doubt passed through various other hands and should be magickally cleansed. I would do this by placing the items under running water, smudging with smoke or placing them underground in suitable wrapping or a container for a night.

As this is a book of flower spells, you will need to find a way to obtain the flowers. Of course the very best way would be to grow them. In the following chapter I will share some ideas and tips on how to do this, but I know it is not possible for everyone to garden, nor is it possible to grow everything in every place all the time.

When purchasing fresh flowers, try and support your local florist and growers. Try your local markets or farmers' markets and look out for local signage. I used to live in a very built-up city area where a lovely lady grew and sold flowers from her suburban backyard.

Selecting fresh flowers should be done with care. Make sure you are purchasing flowers that look and feel energetic and positive and make sure you take them home swiftly and look after them. Remove excess foliage that may turn water brown. Snip stems at an angle to remove dried ends and enable them to easily take a long fresh drink. Place in water with a little sugar or feeder. Change water completely every two to three days and snip stems as required.

One solution to purchasing fresh flowers is to keep dried flowers – something I've been doing successfully for decades and a practice that enables me to have supplies all year round. You easily can dry most flowers by tying in loose bundles and hanging in a cool, dry space. Single blossoms can also be dried on racks or pressed, and for those particularly dedicated there are various food dehydrators on the market that work very well. Another popular flower drying method is the use of silica gel. Flowers are placed in containers layered with the gel in bead form and this dries out flowers over a number of weeks.

Once dry, keep your flowers in a cool, dry place, out of direct sunlight in airtight jars. Label by flower type. You may also like to add place, time or season in which the flower was harvested. Ensure that your flowers are completely dry before bottling or they will grow mould.

Am I Killing the Flower if I Use it in a Spell?

Flowers are part of the lifecycle of plants, which we harvest and enjoy and regrow throughout the year – just like the vegetables you had in your last salad, which may have included parts of plants and maybe also flowers and what could have been flowers taken too soon (put that artichoke down!). You are not killing a flower; you are using a part of a plant at the end of its own lifecycle. To use flowers in spells, be respectful. Don't over harvest, don't uproot whole plants unnecessarily and try to observe the tips I have given above.

❦ GROWING FLOWERS FOR MAGICKAL WORK

A garden, a magickal garden, can be anything from a vast estate to a pot plant. The most important thing is that you grow your flowers organically and with a positive intention. I try and use what I already have and love reusing old containers for pot plants. I'm also a very keen seed swapper and cutting collector.

To teach you how to garden is beyond the scope of this book but I would suggest that you seek out resources close to your home. Your local garden centre not only contains plants to purchase but people who know your area and what will grow there. They will also help you with any challenges you may encounter. Most can also order in plants for you – ones that may not be on display.

Local councils, land and environment bodies, and gardening clubs are all sources of local plant knowledge. The best people of all, however, are your gardening neighbours, who might provide good information about suppliers and other contacts.

When planting flowers, be sure that you are not growing anything that is considered an invasive weed in your area. Be very careful when considering flowers that may be toxic to others, especially wildlife or pets. Planning your garden is important as is soil preparation, seasonal considerations and your climate zone. Below are a few resources to set you on your way to growing your own flowers.

Books

Floret Farm's Cut Flower Garden by Erin Benzakein, Julie Chai and Michele M Waite

The Flower Gardener's Bible by Louis G. Hill and Nancy Hill

The Flower Farmer by Lynn Byczynski

Flower Farmer's Year by Georgie Newbery

Indoor Gardening by Will Cook

Small-Space Container Gardens by Fern Richardson

Websites

The Royal Horticultural Society (UK): www.rhs.org.uk

Gardening Australia: www.abc.net.au/gardening

National Gardening Association (USA): www.garden.org

Kew Gardens: www.kew.org

The Old Farmers Almanac: www.almanac.com

Moon Gardening Guide: www.moongardeningcalendar.com

Horticulture Week: www.hortweek.com

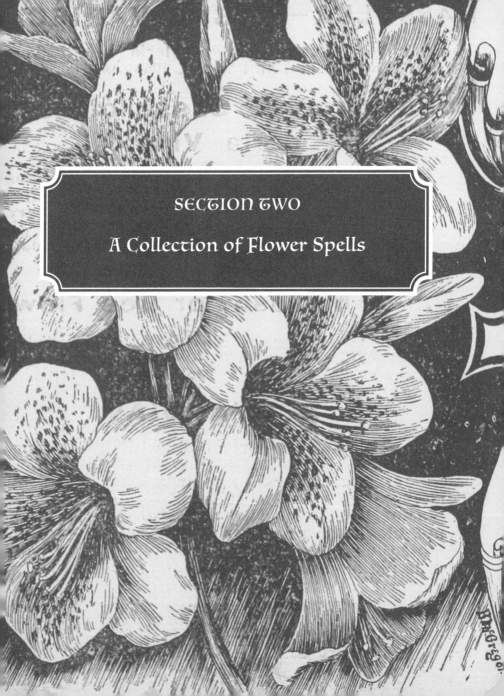

SECTION TWO

A Collection of Flower Spells

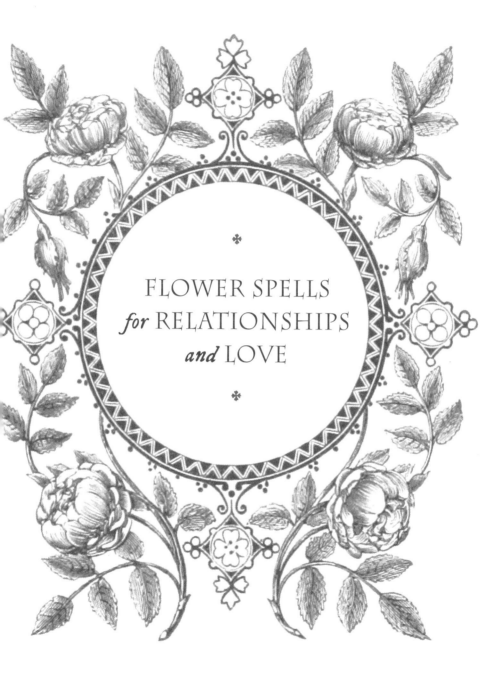

FLOWER SPELLS *for* RELATIONSHIPS *and* LOVE

Lisianthus and Red Rose New Love Spell

If you are looking for a new love, one that will lead to a long-term partnership/relationship/marriage then this spell will help you. Lisianthus will create an atmosphere of desire and open up the possibilities for commitment. Pink and Red Roses will help bring love your way.

Timings

New Moon, Friday, Sunrise

Find and Gather

» a Lisianthus flower (*Eustoma grandiflorium*)
» a Red Rose flower (*Rosa*)
» a red candle
» a pink candle
» a map of an area you would find your new love in (your local area or even the world)

The Spell

Set a protected space and place your map upon a flat surface.

Light your red and your pink candle and place one on either side of your map while imagining the qualities that you would like in your new love.

Gently remove the petals of the Lisianthus and the Rose and let each drift down onto your map until all petals are removed while reciting the following words continuously:

Within the corners of this map,

My new love will be found

Take your petals outside and, dropping them one by one, form a path from your front door. Once you've dropped the last of your petals, walk slowly back and say the following words over and over until you return:

The path is set to bring you to me,

On the steps of roses let our new love now be.

Once your candles have burnt down, take them outside and bury them in the earth. Keep your map and repeat the spell each New Moon until your new love arrives.

Alternate Flowers

Pink Rose *(Rosa)*, Red Carnation *(Dianthus caryophyllus)*, Morning Glory *(Ipomoea purpurea)*, Lady's Mantle *(Alchemilla vulgaris)*, Cornflower *(Centaurea cyanus)*

Lisianthus are native to the prairies of North Western America and so it is no surprise this flower is also known as Prairie Rose.

Mythology tells us that all roses were once white but they became red, stained with the blood of the Goddess Venus after she was pricked with their thorns while trying to save Adonis.

Fuchsia and Agapanthus Rekindle Love Spell

To reconnect with your love you can bake a ring cake, which symbolises the unbroken circle. The element of fire via the heat of the oven will help you light the spark of renewal into a current relationship and can assist with relationships you are attempting to mend. Fuchsia releases emotions and helps people express their true feelings. Agapanthus will affirm your own commitment to love and help prevent the love from fading.

Timings
Full Moon, Sunday, Morning

Find and Gather
»   a Fuchsia flower *(Fuchsia magellanica)*
»   an Agapanthus flower *(Agapanthus praecox)*
»   a ring cake pan (or be prepared to cut a hole
    in the centre of your cake)
»   a favourite cake recipe that you both enjoy
»   a lovely small vase
»   a beautiful pink cloth

The Spell

Make your cake with your loved one, if possible. Set your flowers in their vase next to where you are cooking but do not add these flowers to your mix — they are not edible. Imagine a happier future together while making your cake and, as you do the final mixing, be sure to give it a good stir and say:

Together we blend our hearts,

Together we mend.

Within our new circle,

Love stronger with flame.

Once you have baked your cake, create a beautiful setting upon your pink cloth, which will encourage healing and peaceful and romantic energies to surround you both. Place your vase of flowers in the centre and share your magickal cake together.

Dry your flowers and add to mojo bags, perhaps with a little rose quartz for love.

Place under your pillows at times when you want a little extra spark in your relationship.

Mojo bags are small fabric bags containing magickal items, which are either worn or placed in areas to emit their energies.

If a Bride wears Fuchsias in her hair she will then be assured of the blessings of the Heavens.

The botanical name Agapanthus has a Greek origin: 'Agape', which means love, and 'anthos', meaning flower.

Alternate Flowers

Fuchsia » Poinsettia *(Euphorbia pulcherrima)*, Delphinium *(Delphinium)*

Agapanthus » Ambrosia *(Ambrosia)*, Cactus *(Cactaceae)*

Peruvian Lily and Yellow Rose Friendship Spell

Peruvian Lily helps communicate genuine offers of friendship and expresses devotion to another. Yellow Rose is a flower that not only supports friendships but also helps create space for new beginnings. Creating this offering of refreshments and making a circle is a way of inviting new friends into your life. Make sure you focus on bringing positive souls into your life and go out there in the world to seek them. This spell will help you shine with happy and positive friendship energy.

Timings
Waxing Moon, Friday, Evening

Find and Gather
» a Peruvian Lily *(Alstroemeria)*
» a Yellow Rose *(Rosa)*
» a tiny jar of honey
» a small glass of milk
» a very lovely cupcake/biscuit
» items that represent interests your new friends may share with you

The Spell
Find a welcoming outdoor space and place your treasures, which your new friends may find a common bond with you over, upon the ground. If you love gardening, perhaps you might add a gardening tool; if it is crystals, you could

add your favourite ones; or maybe you want to find friends who share your enthusiasm for animal protection so you might add images of animals.

Holding your flowers, slowly circle your 'friendship treasures' in a clockwise direction, while gently loosening the petals and letting them drift to the earth. Repeat until all petals have been released and your circle is formed. Repeat the following words:

The circle of friendship grows,
New folks I will know.
Good friends of warm heart,
Welcome to our new hearth.

Dip a tiny dash of honey in the milk. Sit and enjoy your milk and sweet treat while imagining your new friendships. You should also be open to messages and ideas that might come to you to help you find avenues to make these lovely new friends.

Once you have finished, gather the petals and bury them under a favourite tree for protection of your spell and future friendships.

Alternate Flowers

Cornflower *(Centaurea cyanus)*, Phlox *(Phlox)*, Shasta Daisy *(Leucanthemum maximum)*, Periwinkle *(Vinca minor)*, Pink Rose *(Rosa)*

The Peruvian Lily is also known as 'The Lily of the Incas'. It has a very long vase-life and can easily last a month.

The Ancient Romans planted roses when a member of the family went away to war or on a long voyage, to ensure their safe return.

Cosmos Communication Improvement Spell

*Cosmos Flowers provide opportunities for communication and coherency.
They also offer peace and tranquility, which is obviously beneficial when
communication is difficult due to raised emotions. This spell is very helpful
at times when you feel you are not being clearly heard by another person/s
or even an institution or company. While you cannot energetically
change their opinion, you can raise energy to ensure you are better
understood so that a fair outcome is more likely.*

Timings
Full Moon, Wednesday, Dusk

Find and Gather
» a small bunch of Cosmos *(Cosmos)*
» two bells
» a blue cloth
» pen and paper
» a clear vase
» a beautiful bottle
» rain/distilled water
» glycerin

The Spell

Lay your cloth out neatly and create a bridge-like pattern with your flowers. This should look roughly like an arch. At either end of the arch, place a bell.

Take out your pen and paper and write whatever it is that you need understood. Be as clear as possible. It is okay to rewrite this a few times until you are happy with it.

Ring the first bell and then say:

Bell, take my words,

Loud, clear and true.

Then read what you have written.

Ring the second bell and say:

So may they be heard

Loud, clear and true.

Place the flowers in a clear vase (this will ensure clarity of your words) with fresh water and place it on top of your message. When the flowers are spent, put them with your folded message into a beautiful bottle with 4/5 rain/distilled water and 1/5 glycerin. Seal the bottle. Whenever you wish your message to be heard, ring a bell and shake your bottle.

Alternate Flowers

Stephanotis *(Stephanotis)*, Delphinium *(Delphinium)*, Hippeastrum *(Hippeastrum)*

Cosmos, comes from the Greek word 'kosmos', which means 'order of the world'.

Originating in Mexico, Spanish explorers carried Cosmos plants across to Spain in in the 16th century. Cosmos flowers have been used since pre-Columbian times to create orange and yellow dyes.

Red Tulip and Rosewater Passion Spell

All Tulips hold the energy of passion, desire and love, but Red Tulips will help those who wish to stoke a passionate fire! They also firmly declare your love for another. In this spell, we will be using rose oil, which has been a favourite passion-inducer throughout history. Cleopatra is said to have had the sails of her barge soaked in rose water before meeting Marc Anthony. Try to find a rhodochrosite crystal for this spell – it really is one of the best for increasing passion. If you can't find one, then a rose quartz will be suitable.

Timings
Full Moon, Friday, Midday

Find and Gather
» a Red Tulip *(Tulipa)*
» rose water
» a rhodochrosite or rose quartz crystal
» a pendant, which you will wear

The Spell
Outside, find a large flat stone. Alternatively, you could use a large flat bowl inside.

Place your rhodochrosite or rose quartz crystal on the rock/in the bowl and place your pendant on it.

Hold your Red Tulip upright over the rock/bowl and slowly fill your tulip with the rose water, letting it run over and onto your crystal and your pendant. All the while, imagine what an increase in passion in your life would look like. Be very specific and really focus on how this energy might come into your life, how you would feel and what you would be doing.

What will you be doing?

What will you feel?

Who are you with?

Picture the scene completely.

Once complete, put the pendant on and keep wearing it until the increase you are searching for occurs in your life. Bury the tulip and the crystal in a place in your garden, or in nature nearby, which the sun shines on for the maximum amount of time each day.

Alternate Flowers

Red Chrysanthemum *(Chrysanthemum)*, Passion Flower *(Passiflora incarnata)*, Red Hibiscus *(Hibiscus rosa-sinensis)*

The black centre of Tulips is said to represent the heart of a lover, darkened by the intense heat of passion.

Tulips are not, as most believe, native to Holland, but from Central Asia. The name comes from the Turkish 'tuliband', which is the material turbans are made from.

Hibiscus and Cyclamen Separation Spell

Cyclamen flowers assist us to say goodbye and to leave a situation cleanly. All Hibiscuses will support your personal, long-term happiness, but White Hibiscus will also provide enlightenment, respect, female healing and, most importantly, help with progression. Cyclamen plants are poisonous, so please take care when using in this spell. Beware of the place you are planting the Cyclamen and keep the flowers out of the reach of young children and pets.

Timings
Waning Moon, Saturday, Midnight

Find and Gather
» a White Hibiscus flower *(Hibiscus)*
» a Cyclamen plant *(Cyclamen)*
» a plant pot and potting mix
» black peppercorns
» mortar and pestle

The Spell
This spell needs to be done in a place you and the person you wish to separate peacefully from have both been to, together.

Gently separate the petals of your White Hibiscus and place them in a circle around your pot. Carefully replant the Cyclamen in the new pot and say:

It is time for goodbye,
I wish us to part,
But peacefully go
and make a new start.

Leave the Cyclamen plant for seven nights and then gift it to the person you are parting with. If you cannot do that, place it at the back door, towards the back of your home, or in the rear yard.

Dry the Hibiscus petals and then grind them with the black peppercorns with the mortar and pestle. This powder is wonderful to use in places where memories of the two of you give rise to unwelcome emotions. Sprinkle a tiny bit of the powder on the ground.

Alternate Flowers

Hibiscus » White Daisy *(Bellis perennis)*, White Carnation *(Dianthus caryophyllus)*

Cyclamen » Calendula *(Calendula officinalis)*

In Hawaii, wearing a Hibiscus behind your right ear indicates you are married; behind your left that you are available; both that you are married but seeking a lover.

Throughout Europe there are many instances of Cyclamen being used in gardens and homes to reverse the power of any spell casting or witchcraft directed against the inhabitants.

Golden Chrysanthemum Pet Protection Spell

*All Chrysanthemums ensure the energy of longevity and happiness, but
Yellow Chrysanthemums also provide a strong boundary against anything
wishing harm. In China, the original place of the Chrysanthemum, mirrors
are used as a magickal means of protection. I have combined both in this
spell for your pets to provide a very powerful combination. For added
protection and deflection of negative energies, grow Chrysanthemums near
the entrance of your home.*

Timings
Waning Moon, Saturday, Midday

Find and Gather
» a Yellow Chrysanthemum *(Chrysanthemum)* for
  each pet
» a small mirror

The Spell
You will need to repeat this spell separately for each pet. You can use the same
mirror but select a new flower for each pet.

Holding the mirror and one Golden Chrysanthemum, walk around your
home as close to the boundary as you can while keeping inside the perimeter.
Then walk through your home, into each and every room and as you do so, say
in each area:

Golden flower of sun,

Shine right and bright for (say your pet's name).

Silver mirror of light,

turn back the dark from (say your pet's name).

Place the mirror in a place that faces the entrance to your home and but one that will still catch the light.

Dry out the Golden Chrysanthemums and bury them near the entrance to your property.

Alternate Flowers

Chrysanthemums of other colours *(Chrysanthemum)*

Chrysanthemum tea originated thousands of years ago, in the Song Dynasty in China. It is said to be beneficial for the heart and, to balance blood pressure. It also acts as a nerve relaxant and is favoured for its high levels of antioxidants.

In Japanese culture, the Chrysanthemum is considered to be symbolic of perfection because of the way the petals carefully unfold.

Baby's Breath Flower Family Harmony Spell

Baby's Breath works to bring harmonic energy into families. It embodies everlasting love and also reminds us to be present and treasure each moment together. As any family member knows, time goes by fast. This special flower helps us breathe, balance ourselves, and enjoy the 'now'. The addition of a moonstone crystal brings peace and calm. These additions can be especially helpful for families experiencing discord or challenging times, and can offer protection. If you are anointing surfaces with the oil, please do a test somewhere inconspicuous first.

Timings
Full Moon, Monday, Morning

Find and Gather
» a sprig of Baby's Breath *(Gypsophila)*
» pure vegetable oil of your choice
» a moonstone crystal
» a clear glass/crystal bowl
» a yellow cloth
» a beautiful bottle
» organic cotton-wool pads or balls

The Spell
In the place in your home most used by your

family, lay out your yellow cloth and place your clear glass/ crystal bowl upon it. Place the moonstone into the bowl and then gently pour your pure vegetable oil into the bowl while breathing softly and deeply over the bowl. This will bring calming energy into the space.

Holding the sprig of Baby's Breath upside-down, use it to stir the oil slowly and trace out the first letter of each member of your family's names with it. Once completed say:

Oil of harmony,

Stone of moon,

Flower of lasting love.

Protect and breathe peace in our family home.

Set the stone aside and pour the oil into the beautiful bottle. You can now instill the energy of harmony by lightly anointing the doorways of each room with the oil or by placing a cotton pad/ball on a dish somewhere in each room of your home. Bury the flowers in your garden and place the moonstone near the place where you created your spell.

Alternate Flowers

Meadowsweet *(Filipendula ulmaria)*

Would you like to attract faeries to your garden? Plant Baby's Breath – it is one of their very favourite flowers.

Originally a Mediterranean plant, the botanical name Gypsophila indicates that it is 'gypsum-loving' meaning it prefers a gypsum-(chalk) rich soil.

Orchid Daily Self-Love Spell

Orchids live very differently to most plants, with many being epiphytes (living anchored on other plants) or occurring rarely and exclusively. All, it can be agreed, are anything but common in habit or appearance. These fascinating flowers are perfect for any spell that focuses on aspects of self-loving, self-esteem and acceptance. The water in this spell assists in calming emotions and opens the bonds between the energies of the Orchid and you. This is a spell you can use daily or when you feel your self-love slipping.

Timings

All Moon Phases, Every Day, Morning

Find and Gather

» a small Orchid plant *(Orchidaceae)*

» a mirror

» a beautiful glass to be used only for this spell

» pure collected or bottled water

The Spell

My suggestion is that you find a place where
you can keep your Orchid in front of a mirror, or that you have a plant small enough to place in front of a mirror. It does not matter if the Orchid is in flower or not – the energy of the flowers is still retained within the plant.

Have your orchid set so that its reflection can be seen along with yours in the mirror. Taking your glass of water, pour a little into the orchid's soil. (Be careful you do not overwater your plant – the tiniest drop will do if you are performing this spell every day.) As you do this, say:

Friend Orchid and I, how different are we,

Not perfect but right for what we may be.

Drink the rest of your water and say:

I celebrate and love,

all that we see.

Take a good moment to really study your Orchid each time you do this spell and see all of its differences from other traditional flowers. Really observe the leaves, the vines or stems and flowers if in bloom – different in many ways, in behavior and form, and yet still serving as a perfect vessel for the spirit of the plant. Much like you.

Alternate Flowers

This spell really requires the energy of Orchids and so as suggested in the introduction to this book, if you really cannot obtain a fresh Orchid plant, I would suggest using a beautifully framed painting or photograph of an Orchid, set before the mirror.

In the Middle East, Orchid tubers are used to create a healing drink called 'Salep', which is said to assist sore throats, digestive problems and gum disease.

Throughout the UK, Orchids have been used in witchcraft as a powerful addition to love potions and spells. They also have a reputation for being able to increase psychic abilities.

Love-in-a-Mist Heart-Healer Spell

*Nigella Flowers are also known as 'Love-in-a-Mist' and they are perfect
for spells that support the healing of broken hearts, and will give you
emotional clarity while doing so. In matters of the heart, they also add a
touch of openness to a new tomorrow.*

Timings
Full Moon, Friday, Midday

Find and Gather
» Love-in-a-Mist flowers *(Nigella damascena)*
» florist wire/wire coat hanger/length of wire
» florist tape/string
» electrical tape/strong tape
» a small hand mirror
» ribbon

The Spell
Find a place where you can see the sun – either outside or inside.

Place and angle your mirror on the ground so it catches the sun. (Be careful
not to shine it into your eyes.) Sit and create a circle from your wire. It does
not need to be large, but you will be adding your flowers to the centre so take
into consideration their size and amount. Overlap each end of your wire circle
and twist together. Cover the join with electrical/strong tape.

Place the circle over you heart and say:

Circle reformed,

Hold gently my heart.

Time will heal and wholeness will be.

Collect your flowers and add to the ring by laying stems on the wire circle and attaching with florist's tape or wire.

Once you have finished creating your flower circle, add a ribbon loop and hang it on your front door or in a window of a favourite room. Use your mirror to shine the sunlight through the center and say:

Sunlight shine again.

Fill my heart with strength and joy,

Sparkling light to my hearth.

Again fill my heart.

When the flowers are spent, you can place them in a mojo bag and hang above your doorway or any window of your home, or you can bury in a sunny spot in the garden.

Alternate Flowers

Pink Gerbera Daisy *(Gerbera)*, Wild Pansy *(Viola tricolor)*

Rich, black Nigella seeds are highly aromatic. This makes them popular in Middle Eastern, Turkish and Indian cuisine as well as for medicinal purposes.

Love-in-a-Mist gained its name from the story of the Emperor Frederick I (1155-1190). He was drowned after being seduced by a green-haired water spirit while on the Third Crusade in the Holy Land.

FLOWER SPELLS *for* HAPPINESS
and HARMONY

Daisy Happiness Spell

How many of us have seen a bunch of daisies or a lawn sprinkled with
their star-like joyfulness and not smiled? Daisies are the very best flowers
of all to engage with should you be seeking happiness in challenging times.
They offer protection and support. This spell creates a lovely, large amount
of Daisy Happiness Bath Fizz. Keep it in lovely glass jars to use later on
too, and to share!

Timings
Full Moon, Friday, Evening

Find and Gather

- » 1 cup of organic dried Daises *(Bellis perennis)* –
  see introduction for tips
- » 1 cup of bath Himalayan/Dead Sea salt
- » 2 cups of Epsom salts
- » 2 cups of baking soda
- » 1 cup of citric acid
- » 1 tablespoon of coconut oil
- » 20 drops of Lemon essential oil
- » a yellow candle
- » a gold cloth
- » a large bowl and wooden spoon
- » a few beautiful airtight jars

The Spell

You can take your bath at any time to enjoy the energy of this spell but it will have added power if you observe the timings suggested when you will ensure maximum happiness power.

Lay out your gold cloth and place all your ingredients upon it. Light your yellow candle and say:

With golden glow and golden light,
Here grows happiness and joyful delight.

With your wooden spoon, mix all of the ingredients together in your large bowl until roughly combined. As you do, repeat:

In mixes smiles, joy and delight,
Love, laughter, happiness
With radiant light.

Make sure in the last eight stirs, you make the infinity sign as you turn the wooden spoon through the bowl. This will impart an infinite happiness blessing. Pot up the mix into your beautiful airtight jars. Use as needed. Half a cup is usually sufficient for a bath.

Alternate Flowers

There are no substitutions for Daisies for this particular spell.

'Daisy' comes from the old English term 'Day's Eye', referring to the way daisies open with the rising sun and close when it sets.

Creating and wearing daisy chains was seen as a way to protect you from you being carried away by faeries.

Poppy Painful Memory Healing Spell

*Poppies instill rest and peace while also connecting us with memories.
They help us heal painful memories with their additional calming
influences. Poppies also help us in our dream state; so if your memories
are affecting your sleep, you may find this spell brings sweeter dreams.
The addition of fresh rosemary will also assist with the cleansing
of negative memories.*

Timings
Waning Moon, Wednesday, Midday

Find and Gather
» a bunch of Poppies *(Papaver)*
» a length of orange ribbon
» a large bowl
» bubble wand or a wire coat hanger bent into a circle shape
» a sprig of fresh rosemary/wooden spoon to stir

To make the Magickal Bubble Mix:
» ½ cup of dishwashing detergent
» ¼ cup of glycerin
» 1 cup of warm water

The Spell

Combine all the ingredients of the Magickal Bubble Mix into the bowl and stir lightly with the sprig of rosemary/wooden spoon and say:

> *Memories which pain me,*
> *Swirl and away.*
> *With each drifting bubble,*
> *May they heal and fade today.*

With the orange ribbon, tie your poppies to a tree branch or in a high spot outside.

Dip your bubble wand or wire circle into the Magickal Bubble Mix and blow bubbles around, through, over and under your poppies. As you do, think of each memory and moment you want to ease as being inside the bubbles you are blowing. Capture them in a bubble and let them drift away.

The best way to release the poppies you have used is to cast them upon moving water (the sea, a stream, river or creek). You can bottle your Magickal Bubble Mix to use again.

Alternate Flowers

Zephyr Lily *(Zephyranthes)*, Cherokee Rose *(Rosa laevigata)*

In the folklore of many cultures, it is believed that if one stares into the centre of a poppy before bedtime, a deep, peaceful sleep is assured.

It was the Battle of Waterloo, and the subsequent blooming of poppies after the fighting, which began the belief that poppies sprung from the blood of the fallen, as a token of remembrance.

Daffodil Hope Renewal Spell

Not only do Daffodils express hope for the future, they are also bringers of sunshine, inspiration, renewal and vitality. If you like, you can add crystals and items that have similar energies to this mist mixture. This is a very good spell to experiment with when writing your own spells. Find flowers that hold energies, via their meanings, that you wish to bring into your life and tailor the chants to suit. When the mist runs out, cast the spell again.

Timings
Waxing Moon, Sunday, Morning

Find and Gather

» 3 Daffodil flowers *(Narcissus pseudonarcissus)*
» a clear glass or crystal bowl (it is preferable to obtain a bowl you will use only for making the essences)
» a cup of pure water
» misting bottle
» a purple cloth

The Spell
Find a place, preferably outside, where
you can leave your essence for an hour in the sunlight. Lay your purple cloth

neatly and place your clear glass/crystal bowl upon it. Slowly pour your pure water into it and say:

Sparkle water,

Dance in the sun.

Take in the joy,

a new day begun.

Put your flowers into the water one by one. The flowers only need to have parts of their petals touching or in the water – they do not need to be fully immersed. As you place each flower into the water say each time:

I welcome sunshine.

I welcome happiness.

I embrace hope.

Leave your essence water and flowers in the sunlight for an hour and then strain into your misting bottle. Use each morning in the air of your space (home/work) and repeat the above chant each time. The flowers should be buried in a spot that always has sunshine upon it.

Alternate Flowers

German Iris *(Iris germanica)*, Petunia *(Petunia)*

In Wales, it is said that the person who finds the first Daffodil blossom in Spring will have 'more gold than silver over the next year'.

Never display a single Daffodil in your home. Whether it is a fresh flower or an image, ensure it is a bunch. It is very bad luck otherwise.

White Lily and Rose Truth Spell

If you are trying to cut through deception or hazy information and find the truth, then the pure White Lily and Rose will assist you. Both of these flowers are not only vessels of truth but they are also protective flowers that can help you on your quest.

Timings
New Moon, Wednesday, Night

Find and Gather

» 1 White Lily *(Lilium)*
» 1 White Rose *(Rosa)*
» white ribbon – about 60 cm/24" in length
» white sheet of paper – ensure it is completely clean, unmarked and without creases

The Spell
Snip the stems of both flowers so they are about 5cm/2" long.

Lie flowers next to each other – you can pop the Rose into the Lily if it small enough and bind together by winding the white ribbon around the stems of the flowers. Tie three knots on top of each other at the end of the stems so you form almost a thick ball.

Hold this ribbon ball loosely between your thumb and forefinger of your dominant hand above the white paper.

Ask questions that you already know the answers to and have firm yes or no answers. For example, you can ask: 'Is my car blue?' or 'Is my dog's name Sundar?' or 'Do I have nine children?' Ask lots of questions and take close note of what happens to your Flower Pendulum. How does it move in relation to the answer? You should come to see that a 'no' answer will give you a different movement to a 'yes' answer. It could be a rocking movement in a certain direction or a circle in one direction or another.

Once you have deciphered how your flowers will answer, settle yourself by clearing your mind and grounding yourself again. Ask your Flower Pendulum to stop before you begin by saying:

Rest and be still.

You may like to say 'stop' as is popular with many who use pendulums.

After you obtain your answers, tie the Flower Pendulum to a tree branch and say:

Thank you for the truth.

I now set you free.

Alternate Flowers

It really is preferable that you do not substitute flowers in this spell. If you cannot obtain one of the flowers, then use two of the type you do have.

St Thomas did not believe that the Virgin Mary had ascended after her death so he ordered her tomb be opened. All that was within where Lilies and Roses, which has led to their connection, to this day, with her image in artworks.

Carrying fresh Lilies will ensure that any love spell cast upon you will be broken. This probably led to their popularity in bridal bouquets.

Frangipani Self-Confidence Spell

Using Frangipani in this spell will not only increase your self-confidence but will give you freedom to happily be your true self. Use the timings below in the creation of your Flower Spell Box as this will empower it. You can open it any time you need a boost in self-confidence.

Timings
Waxing Moon, Sunday, Midday

Find and Gather
» a Frangipani *(Plumeria alba)*
» a plain small wooden box with a lid
» white fabric bag or cloth to place box in
» a piece of rose quartz
» a photo of yourself

The Spell
First dry your flower completely using one of the methods described in the introduction to this book.

Place your flower and all the other items listed in the spell into your box and say:

In you go, one by one.

Mix together.

You have work to do.

Close the box lid and say:

Magickal box,

Confidence build.

Each time you open, my spell will fulfill.

Put your Flower Spell Box in the white fabric bag/cloth and find a dark, quiet place to keep it.

When you would like the magick of your spell to assist in boosting your self-confidence, simply open the Flower Spell Box and say:

Magickal box,

Confidence build.

Now you are open, my spell will fulfill.

You can use this Flower Spell Box forever, but if you feel at any time that it is no longer working for you, bury it and create another.

Alternate Flowers

Yellow Hibiscus *(Hibiscus)*, Poet's Narcissus *(Narcissus poeticus)*

It is believed in many cultures throughout Asia that Frangipani trees are home to ghosts. In Malaysia, the scent is said to accompany the appearance of the Pontianak – a female vampire.

To the Mayan Lakandon people, the gods were born from Frangipani flowers.

Hyacinth Tension-Relief Spell

Hyacinth flowers are all about playfulness, letting things go, games, sport and generally being free. In this spell we are getting a little arty/ crafty, in order to connect with the energy of your flower and capture it in a gorgeous little charm bag to carry with you. If you have glitter pens, scented markers and the like, then use them – Hyacinths really do love a bit of fun. This spell is especially helpful for days when you feel general tension but can also be used when you know you are going into a high-tense situation.

Timings
Waning Moon, Friday, Evening

Find and Gather

» 1 Hyacinth *(Hyacinthus)*
» a vase
» a beautiful tiny bag
» a piece of paper to draw on
» a pencil
» colouring pens or pencils
» music that makes you happy

The Spell
Set your fresh Hyacinth before you in the vase.

Play your music – anything that makes you feel happy and carefree. Make sure it stays on for the entire spell. You might like to either put a song on a loop or play a selection of music.

Take out your paper and pens/pencils and draw your Hyacinth flower. Have fun and do not worry about the end result. In fact, the more loose, crazy, colourful and fun you can make your picture, the better. Do not judge what you are doing – just relax, scribble, doodle and get lost in creating, colouring and releasing lines on paper while your music plays.

Once you are finished and when your artwork is dry (if you used paint), hold it up to your Hyacinth flower and say:

Hop into my picture, sweet flower,
Now come dance around.
Please leave playfulness, tension release,
and your own magick sound.

Fold the artwork three times and place it into your beautiful little bag. Carry it with you to offer relief and protection in tense times. When needed, close your eyes and place the bag next to your ear for a few moments. Once your Hyacinth has spent, bury it in a cool dark place in the garden/Nature.

Alternate Flowers

Ginger *(Zingiber officinale)*, German Chamomile *(Matricaria chamomilla)*

A growing Hyacinth in a pot or bulb vase will ease nightmares. The perfume will work to dissipate negative feelings.

Hyacinths are said to have made their way to Holland via a shipwreck off the coast of the Netherlands in the 18th century. Locals planted the expensive bulbs which had originally been bound for medicinal use in European cities.

Gerbera Daisy Blues Busting Spell

Feeling low? Especially if you cannot put your finger on exactly what is causing you to feel negative vibes, this spell with the inclusion of Gerberas will not only bring a burst of positivity, the onions will absorb negativity.

Timings
Waning Moon, Sunday, Midnight

Find and Gather
» 8 Gerbera Daisies *(Gerbera jamesonii)*
» an onion
» rubber gloves
» a knife
» a clear bowl of pure water
» 4 small vases

The Spell
Cut your onion into quarters, leaving the skin on, and place one quarter in each corner of your bedroom. Carefully lay a Gerbera Daisy in front of each onion quarter, with the stem close but not touching the onion and with the flower pointing towards the centre of the room.

GERBERA
HYBRIDS.

Leave overnight.

The Gerbera Daisies will attract all the negativity to the onions, where it will be absorbed.

Next morning collect all the onion quarters while wearing the rubber gloves – you do not wish to absorb back any energy yourself. Chop up the onions and bury in your garden/Nature in a sun-filled area.

Collect the Gerberas, still wearing the gloves, and immerse in the bowl of pure water. Leave in the sunlight for an hour and then, thanking them for their work, bury them in another sun-filled area away from the onions.

The next night, place each of the remaining Gerbera Daisies in a separate, small vase, and place in the areas you had the onions quarters the night before.

Leave them there until they are spent. They will emit all of their positive vibes into your space until they are spent. Once spent, bury in another sun-filled area of your garden/Nature.

Alternate Flowers

Buttercup *(Ranunculus acris)*, Shasta Daisy *(Leucanthemum maximum)*

Gerbera Daisies originate from Transvaal, South Africa, near Barberton. They are mostly known in that country as Transvaal Daisies or Barberton Daisies.

Gerbera Daisies are now the fifth most popular cut flower in the world after Roses, Carnations, Chrysanthemum and Tulips.

Wild Rose and Geranium Stop Gossip Spell

*Wild Rose makes up an important part of this spell because it is one
of the great flowers of truth. It helps uncover the truth as well as any
betrayal that has occurred. It also opens a new path open for you to move
on. Geranium is included in this spell because it offers comfort and helps
you rise in elegance and grace above any gossip about you.*

Timings
Waning Moon, Saturday, Dusk

Find and Gather

- » 1 Wild Rose *(Rosa acicularis)*
- » 1 Geranium *(Geranium)*
- » 11 drops of Rose Geranium essential oil
- » 1 cup of sea salt
- » approximately ½ cup of sweet almond oil
- » an airtight glass jar

The Spell
Use the timings above to create your spell, but you can use your magickal salt
scrub ingredients (above) at any time.

Dry a handful of each flower using the methods shared in the first section
of this book.

Add the salt and flowers to the jar and stir well.

Pour the oil into the jar in small amounts and mix as you go. Stop when you achieve the consistency you desire. You may like a wetter or drier mix and so may use more or less of the oil.

Add the Rose Geranium essential oil and stir through your mix.

When required: Before use, stir your mix with a wood spoon so the consistency is even.

You can either add a handful to a warm bath and soak, or use as a scrub in the shower.

If you are worried about gossip, then a warm bath is better as it will envelope you in a protective veil. However, if you are aware of particular gossip, then visualise it bouncing off you and disappearing down the drain while you use your scrub.

Alternate Flowers

Any type of Rose or Geranium can be used in this spell.

Faeries can become invisible by eating a Wild Rose hip and then turning counterclockwise three times. By eating another and turning clockwise, they become visible again.

Many Geraniums are beautifully scented. Layer sugar with the leaves in airtight jars for a few weeks. Discard the leaves and you will be left with delightfully scented sugar to use in drinks, teas and cooking.

Iris and Passion Flower Inspiration Spell

The Iris in this spell not only connects you with inspirational energies, it will strengthen faith and clear away negative feelings. Passion Flower holds exactly what its name suggests – passion! The flower also offers pathways to your higher consciousness that could assist you in seeking new inspiration.

Timings
Full Moon, Wednesday, Dusk

Find and Gather
» 1 Iris flower *(Iris versicolor)*
» 1 Passion Flower *(Passiflora incarnata)*
» a stone
» a clear glass/crystal bowl
» pure water

The Spell
Go for a walk in Nature – a park, a garden, the beach – on the day of a Full Moon, and wait until a smooth stone, which you know you can easily carry in your pocket or bag with you anywhere, appears in your path. Take the stone to running water. This could be the sea, a river or creek. Hold the stone under the water to cleanse it. The running water will release any negative emotions that can block inspiration. Pour your pure water

in the clear glass/crystal bowl and then add your Iris and say:

And you are for inspiration,

The thoughts which excite,

Add your Passion Flower and say:

And you are for passion,

The fire that creates.

Add your stone and say:

Inspiration and passion,

A new touchstone fashioned.

Take out your stone, gently dry and leave it out in the moonlight for the evening.

In the morning, your Inspiration Touchstone will be ready for you. Take it with you whenever you wish and hold it and rub it between your fingers when you are seeking inspiration. Repeating the above spell can recharge your Touchstone if needed. Cast spent flowers upon running water.

Alternate Flowers

For either flower: Daffodil *(Narcissus pseudonarcissus)*, Bee Orchid *(Ophrys apifera)*, Red Tulip *(Tulipa)*

Iris flowers are named after the Goddess Iris, of the rainbow. Her role was to guide women to the Elysian Fields and this is why planting Irises on women's graves has been popular throughout history.

Growing Passion Flower at the entrance to your house will ensure no harm enters.

Camellia and Freesia Calm Spell

You can use this spell at any time to bring calm to you or into a space. It is a very good spell to use after times of stress. Create it using the timings below, bottle it up and keep in your apothecary. Soft, blousy Camellias lend their calmness and promise of peace while Freesia assures trust while showing you inner guidance so that you may feel more hopeful and balanced. Use a leaf to sprinkle the water to emulate the gentleness of calming rain. Collect your rainwater, preferably during a Full or Waning Moon. If you don't have any rainwater, use the purest water you can find.

Timings
Full Moon, Friday, Midnight

Find and Gather

» 3 Camellia flowers *(Camellia japonica)*
» 3 Freesia flowers *(Freesia)*
» a clear glass/crystal bowl
» rainwater
» a large leaf

The Spell
Half fill your glass/crystal bowl with rainwater

Place your Camellias in your bowl, one by one, and with each say:

Calm and calmer.

Now place each of your Freesias in your water and say:

Balance and balanced.

You can use this mixture straight away or bottle with 1/5 glycerin to preserve for use at any time. Spent flowers should be buried in a dark part of the garden/Nature.

To use, pour a little mixture into a clear glass bowl and dip a fresh leaf into it. Walk around the area you wish to bring calm to, and gently flick the leaf to sprinkle a tiny amount of the mixture into the air. You can also do this around yourself or another person for the same effect.

Alternate Flowers

Camellia » Flannel Flower *(Actinotus helianthi)*, Rose Geranium *(Pelargonium graveolens)*

Freesia » Jasmine *(Jasminum officinale)*, Daffodil *(Narcissus pseudonarcissus)*

Camellias can also attract money. Place with another plant near the entrance of your home or in a fresh bowl inside.

Freesias are the flower for 7th wedding anniversaries. With their energy of trust, hope and balance, they may be just the thing for avoiding the 7-year itch.

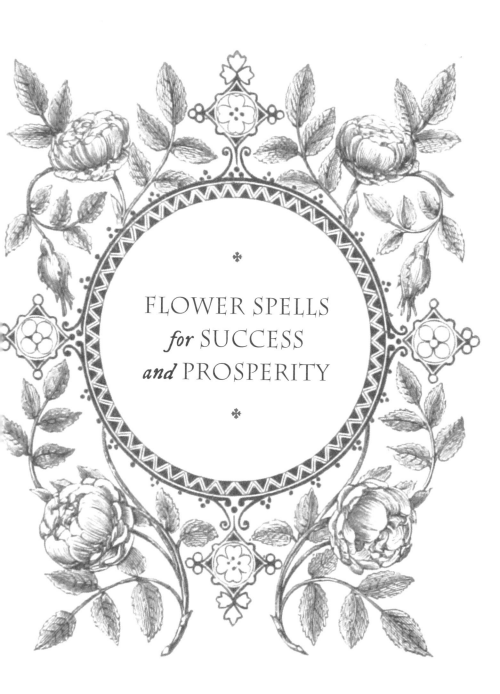

FLOWER SPELLS *for* SUCCESS *and* PROSPERITY

Nasturtium Goal-Setting Spell

This spell will help you set and strengthen new goals to ensure the maximum chances of success. If your belief in your ability to attain your goals is strong from the beginning, then you are more likely to stick with what is needed to succeed.

Timings
Waxing Moon, Thursday, Sunrise

Find and Gather
» a plant pot and potting mix (or a place to plant, in the garden)
» a green candle in a holder
» Nasturtium *(Tropaeolum majus)* seedling or seeds
» white paper
» a green pen

The Spell
Using your preferred method, create protection for the space where you are planting your flower – the pot or area where your plant will reside.

Write your goal on the piece of paper and read out loud three times, then bury it in the soil, in the same place where you will plant your seed/s or plant.

Plant your seed/s or plant and, as you do, recite the following, three times:

Flower, hear my goals and grow.

Take them with you as you go.

Water your plant seed/s and then release energy, by clapping your hands three times and acknowledging that the spell is done. Ground yourself by placing your hands on the earth.

If possible, let the green candle burn down outside. Make sure you attend it at all times. If you cannot stay with it, bury it next to your plant or seed/s.

Make sure you look after your plant to encourage the success of your goals.

Alternate Flowers

Buttercup *(Ranunculus acris)*, Pink Heath *(Epacris impressa)*, Amaryllis *(Amaryllis)*

Nasturtiums are edible. The leaves and flowers have a pepper-like flavour and can be used in salads and sandwiches as well as a flavouring for oils, dressings and butters. The immature seeds can be pickled and used in place of capers.

Common Nasturtiums are native to Peru. Their botanical name, 'Tropaeolum', comes from the Latin for 'shield' referring to the shape of their leaves.

Delphinium Make-Things-Happen Spell

Please note that all Delphiniums are poisonous to humans and animals. The ability of these flowers to make things possible, however, makes them a powerful ally in this spell. But you are advised to carefully use and release. You may wish to use gloves to handle these flowers as some people experience mild skin irritations.

For the 'bunch of flowers' used in this spell, go out and pick or purchase a bunch of flowers that you feel drawn to. You will be using their petals to make a mandala, so be mindful of their suitability for this task.

Timings
Waxing Moon, Tuesday, Daytime

Find and Gather
» a bunch of Delphinium flowers *(Delphinium)*
» another bunch of flowers that you are drawn to
» a picture or an object that describes what it is you wish to make happen
» a large purple cloth
» a smaller gold cloth
» 12 sunflower seeds
» 4 golden candles

The Spell

Lay your purple cloth out and place your smaller gold one upon it.

Place your golden candles in each corner of the gold cloth (North, South, East and West) and place three sunflower seeds in front of each candle. Place the picture or object that best describes what it is you wish to happen in the centre of the gold cloth. Arrange the Delphinium flowers closely on or around the picture or object.

Separate the petals of the flowers that you have collected and create a mandala around your Delphiniums and treasures. To do this, simply work in growing circles around your centre collection. Although you can be as creative as you wish, the energy to make this spell work comes from your focused concentration on the things you wish to happen, not on your artistic abilities. Once you are finished (take as long as you like), light your candles and say:

> *Circle of petals,*
> *Dance into life.*
> *These treasures you hold*
> *With Delphinium tonight.*

Let your candles burn down safely and leave your mandala for a day and night before putting away. Bury the flowers and petals under a tree you really love, with a small token that represents your desires. Plant the sunflower seeds.

Alternate Flowers

Delphinium » Hippeastrum *(Hippeastrum)*, Crowea *(Crowea exalata)*

In many countries Delphinium are also know as Larkspur. This is because one of the petals of its flower points backwards like a spur.

Delphinium was used by Ancient Greek soldiers to help control body lice.

African Violet Study and Exam Spell

Although African Violets are traditionally connected with spiritual learning,
they are also very helpful if you are studying – especially at exam time.
African Violets also offer personal protection at these times so you are able
to do your best work free from additional challenges. If you can, choose a
yellow pot to plant your flower. Yellow is the colour of learning, intellect,
memory and mental clarity. If you cannot find a yellow pot try painting one
or tie a yellow ribbon around your pot. If you cannot find individual fluorite
crystal beads, you can use a ready-made bracelet. Simply take the bracelet
apart and then restring as the spell instructs.

Timings
Waxing Moon, Wednesday, Morning

Find and Gather
»   1 African Violet plant *(Saintpaulia)*
»   a yellow plant pot
»   appropriate potting mix
»   a collection of fluorite crystal beads,
    enough to circle your wrist
»   beading elastic

The Spell

Make sure your plant is healthy. It does not need to be in flower, however – the energy of the flowers is always right through the plants they spring from.

Plant your African Violet into your yellow pot. As you complete the task say:

Wise violet sit with me,
From this day on.
Enhance my study and knowledge
So my mind remains strong.

'Plant' your fluorite beads around your African Violet. Count them and do not bury so deep that they are difficult to retrieve. Leave them overnight and 'harvest' the next morning.

Rinse the fluorite beads under running water and thread onto your beading elastic. I would suggest you thread onto two strands to ensure added strength Wear when you are studying and when undertaking exams.

To recharge at any time, place on the soil next to the African Violet.

Alternate Flowers

There are no substitutes for this spell.

African Violet plants enhance spirituality while offering protection within a home.

New plants can be grown from a leaf of an African Violet plant. One 'mother' leaf will grow approximately 6–16 'babies'. Once the tiny plants have an established root system, you can repot.

Stargazer Lily Business Protection and Success Spell

This flower will open up new opportunities, invite abundance and prosperity and support ambition. Florida Water is a cologne made from flowers and herbs. It is traditionally used to magickally cleanse and protect either a person or space. For many communities, especially those connected with the practice of Vodon, it is a powerful spiritual protector and cleanser.

Do not drink this water — it is to be sprayed lightly as a personal fragrance, added to a bath or sprinkled around your place of business.

Timings
Waxing Moon, Thursday, Daytime

Find and Gather
» small handful of Pink Stargazer Lily petals (*Lilium orientalis*) dried as per instructions at the start of this book
» 2 cups of vodka
» 2 tablespoons of orange-flower water
» 2 drops of jasmine essential oil
» 16 drops of bergamot essential oil
» 12 drops of lavender essential oil
» 3 drops of lemon essential oil

» 2 drops of rose attar essential oil

» a gorgeous bottle

The Spell

Make sure you use the timings to create your Business-Protection-and-Success Water to add a bigger boost when you are finding times particularly challenging.

Mix all ingredients together and bottle.

Sprinkle in the area where you work – such as your office – or dab a little on yourself. Use as needed to provide protection and to ensure success to your business endeavours.

You may find it useful to use the water at the beginning of your working week and again at times when you are attending important meetings, undertaking decision making and working on anything especially challenging.

Before using as a fragrance on your skin, do a small patch test on your inner arm first and monitor for 24 hours.

Adding to a spray bottle can also make it easier to use.

Alternate Flowers

Stargazer Lily is the very best flower to use for this particular spell. If you really need to substitute, try Peruvian Lily (*Alstroemeria*).

Stargazer Lilies were bred by Leslie Woodriff, in California in 1974. He called the new cross 'Stargazer', because the blooms faced towards the sky.

Although many people adore the fragrance of Stargazer Lilies, a percentage find the scent completely repulsive.

Carnation Decision Maker Spell

Carnations cannot make a decision for you but they can help by offering clarity to help you find ways to progress, achieve positive outcomes and also support your life-force while doing so. By creating a spell bottle, you are emulating the cloudiness you may feel with your decision-making. The cloudiness when the bottle is shaken will be like all the pieces mixed up in your own personal puzzle. Watching the contents naturally settle will help you to become similarly aligned and see a balanced picture. This will help you to make your decision.

You can obtain tiny corked bottles easily from craft stores and online. Some come with pendant fittings already attached should you wish to wear your bottle.

Timings
Waxing Moon, Wednesday, Dusk

Find and Gather
- » ½ cup of dried Red Carnation petals
  (Dianthus caryophyllus)
- » 2 tablespoons of rose water
- » a piece of jade stone
- » a beautiful clear bottle and seal
- » water

The Spell

Divide the dried Red Carnation petals into two piles and set before your bottle.

Pick a few petals from each the pile – one for each hand. At the same time, say:

One hand for this way,

The other for that.

Add them to your bottle and say:

Together please help me

So I see where I'm at.

Add your rose water and say:

With love to guide me

Add your jade stone and say:

And clear sight ahead.

Seal your bottle and whenever you are seeking clarity to make a decision, simply shake your bottle and sit quietly and watch the contents completely settle. You should receive thoughts that will help you, or at least calm you, and clear your vision, to move forward.

Alternate Flowers

There are no alternatives for this spell.

Spell bottles are also known as witch bottles and have been in use since at least the early 17th century in the UK and USA.

The name Carnation is thought to come from the word 'coronation' as the flowers were used as ceremonial headdresses in Ancient Greece.

Dandelion Wishing Spell

Dandelion flowers are the yellow tufted daisy-like blossoms that precede the dainty seed balls that we usually pluck from our lawns to make a wish. Dandelions have many health benefits and their use as such has been recorded since at least Ancient Persia. In this spell, we are connecting with the Dandelions' additional energies and reputation to make wishes come true. I would suggest you find a lovely vintage or new teapot and cup that you can use solely for this spell. Energetically cleanse it using one of the spells at the beginning of this book and empower it by leaving it filled with water under a Full Moon for a night.

Dandelion

Timings
Waxing, Thursday, Daytime

Find and Gather
» 11 organic Dandelion flowers (*Taraxacum officinale*), fresh or dried
» boiling water
» honey (optional)
» lemon juice (optional)
» a beautiful teapot and cup

The Spell

Place your Dandelion flowers into your teapot and say:

Flowers of wishes,

Flowers of light,

Into the pot

May my wishes be right.

Pour in the boiling water and say:

Dance in the water,

Dance with delight.

The person who drinks you

Has wishes in sight.

Turn the teapot three times clockwise while saying your wish out loud and then pour your cup of tea and say:

Now that I drink you,

My wishes come true.

Thank you sweet flower,

For all that you do.

Alternate Flowers

There are no alternatives for this spell.

Blowing the seeds from a Dandelion and making a wish is a long-lived English folk practice. Blowing the Dandelion helps the faeries to spread the seeds and, in doing so, granting our wish to us.

Dandelion root can be ground and used as a healthy substitute for coffee. This hot brew is also said to increase your psychic powers.

Water Lily Psychic Ability Spell

You will not necessarily need a fresh Water Lily for this spell — you can use one in dried form. With roots in the earth, stems and leaves weaving through the water, this flower sits aloft in the air, under the gaze of the sun, connecting all elements — above to below — and everything between the worlds.

Water Lily reminds us that all is connected, no matter where we find ourselves or in what state. Use this spell at each New Moon to increase your psychic abilities. While you are using the spell for this purpose, you may receive messages.

Timings
New Moon, Monday, Late Night

Find and Gather
» 1 Water Lily *(Nymphaeaceae)* or a handful of dried Water Lily petals
» a beautiful purple cloth
» a deep, large bowl
» pure water
» a green candle
» a blue candle
» a red candle

» a yellow candle

» pen and journal

The Spell

Place your purple cloth on a surface (such as a table). This represents 'spirit'. Rest your bowl on your cloth and half fill with water.

Place each of your candles around the bowl according to your hemisphere. Usual placement is: Earth – North (green), Fire – South (red), Air – East (yellow), Water – West (blue). You may like to reverse to suit the Southern Hemisphere or your geographic location, to correspond with the geography of the land. Light your candles. Float your Water Lily or cast your dried petals upon the water and say:

Above and below, from the East and the West,

Flower of all now come to rest.

Flower divine, from below to above,

Help me to see with truth and with love.

Ideally, you should stay with your spell until all candles burn down. Take notes of patterns, thoughts, visions and feelings. Once the candles have burned down, discard all spell items by burying them in a part of your garden in the direction of the next Full Moon.

Alternate Flowers

There are no alternative flowers for this spell.

The name of the plant gene 'Nymphaea' contains the word 'nymph', which describes those elemental beings who inhabit waterways.

The perfume of Water Lilies is said to be restorative and healing.

Gladiolus Creativity Success Spell

Gladiolus support those who are looking for success, particularly in the creative arts. They really are the very best flower to give to those enjoying an opening night, a book launch or an exhibition opening, for example. These flowers encourage people to never give up on their dreams; they encourage a healthy ego and support creative growth.

GLADIOLA

Timings
Full Moon, Friday, Daytime

Find and Gather
» 1 stem of Gladiolus (*Gladiolus)*
» an example of your creative work (a painting/ drawing or photograph of you dancing or performing in a play, some music or a sheet of music to play, for example)
» a teaspoon
» a small and very beautiful container
» a tiny, silk copper- or gold-coloured drawstring bag

The Spell
Select nine petals from your Gladiolus and dry them according to the instructions at the front of this book.

You must do this spell on a Full Moon for it to work.

Take your creative work and sit on the ground and work on it or interact with it for as long as you like – you could draw, paint, write, play music, dance or act out a scene, whatever it is that you wish to increase success in. Make sure that whatever you do is your true passion and that you are comfortable and can enjoy yourself.

Collect a teaspoon of the earth from where you were creating. Mix it with your dry Gladiolus petals and crumble together.

Place this earth in your small container and put the container in your small silk bag.

To use, take out of the silk bag and sprinkle the mix on the spot you are performing or creating in.

To attract the success to your home/office/studio, repeat the spell above but collect ¼ cup of earth and dry 27 petals to make your mix. Sprinkle the mixture from the road to your front door and hang some in a tiny silk bag in the centre of your studio space or your bedroom.

Alternate Flowers

Fairy Iris *(Dietes grandiflora)*, Wisteria *(Wisteris sinensis)*

A 'gladius' is a sword of Ancient Roman Legionnaires, while a shorter sword was a 'gladiolus' and the word 'Gladiator', describes those who lived by the sword.

Most parts of Gladiolus plants are poisonous but they have been used throughout time in medicine, especially the corms in the extraction of splinters, thorns and drawing out infection.

Scotch Thistle Flower Find-What-is-Lost Spell

A Scotch Thistle flower holds the energy of integrity, truth and pride, and so is a powerful ally to assist in ensuring what is rightfully yours is returned to you. Be very careful that what it is that you have lost is yours – Scotch Thistle has a nasty sting for those working with the energy of retaliation or dishonesty. Sunflower seeds offer light and strength for your quest.

In this spell you will be placing beeswax under your pillow so I would suggest that you not only place it into the cloth listed but encase the entire spell in something else to protect your bed linen from any staining.

Timings
New Moon, Monday, Midnight

Find and Gather

» Scotch Thistle Flower *(Onopordum acanthium)*
» 6 sunflower seeds
» a sheet of beeswax
» a scribing tool
» a thick piece of purple fabric

The Spell
On a sheet of beeswax draw/write about what it is that you have lost. Be as descriptive as possible.

Place your Scotch Thistle flower in the centre of your beeswax sheet and say:

Flower of truth,

help return what is mine.

Place each of your sunflower seeds around the Scotch Thistle and with each say:

Seeds of the sun,

Light the place (say what it is you are looking for) *resides.*

Roll the beeswax up and wrap it in the purple cloth. Place it under your pillow.

You should hopefully dream of where your object is or what has become of it, or it will be revealed to you during the day.

Alternate Flowers

Snapdragon *(Antirrhinum majus)*, Iris *(Iris)*

The Thistle has been a popular heraldic symbol throughout history and was first documented used by King James III of Scotland (1452–1488).

A Thistle worn in any form, either fresh or in textile design or jewelry, has long been considered a powerful protective symbol.

Yellow Rose New-Beginning Spell

Rose petal beads are traditionally created from either funeral flowers and
called 'Memorial Beads' or from bridal flowers and called 'Memory Beads'.
In this spell, you will be creating Rose petal beads and instilling them with
hope and positivity for a new beginning. Wearing them will remind you
of commitments made as you move forward in life and they will be very
helpful to counter any challenges you face along the way. Yellow Roses
welcome and support new beginnings, hold promises of returns and are
particularly powerful in any spell work involving friends.

Timings
Waxing Moon, Sunday, Midday

Find and Gather
» 9 Yellow Roses *(Rosa)* – old-
  fashioned ones are preferable
» 3 Red Roses *(Rosa)* – old-fashioned
  are preferable
» pure water
» rose essential oil
» mortar and pestle
» baking paper and tray
» nails or pins the thickness you wish the bead holes to be
» a piece of styrofoam

The Spell

Pluck the petals from the Roses and with the mortar and pestle grind them until they are broken down as much as possible. Spread your crushed Roses out on baking paper on trays to dry for a day.

Once dried, return the petals to your mortar and pestle and grind again, but add a small amount of water to help form a paste. Ideally you will want to work the mix as much as possible in order to make most of the small pieces in your mix 'disappear' into the dough. Make sure you end up with thick dough. If the mix is too thin, it won't set easily.

Next you will roll the beads. The size of your beads is totally up to you. Coat your fingers in rose oil and roll the petal dough mixture into the size and shape you wish your beads to be, as you do say:

Yellow Rose, light my way,

A new beginning, starts today.

Thread each bead onto a nail/pin and push into styrofoam. Place in a sunny position to dry completely. This can take a few days. Once fully dried, thread your bead onto beading thread, elastic and ribbon. You can wear the beaded necklace whenever you wish, or hang in your home above a doorway or window near the front entrance to your home.

Alternate Flowers

White Rose *(Rosa)*, Yellow Chrysanthemum *(Chrysanthemum)*

Up until the 18th century, no one outside the Middle East had ever seen a Yellow Rose. The Yellow Rose caused much excitement in Europe at the time of its discovery.

If you want to ask someone to give you another chance, give them a bunch of Yellow Roses.

FLOWER SPELLS *for* PROTECTION *and* CLEARING

Triple Rose Smudging Spell

Smudge sticks work by collecting negativity in their smoke and whisking it away. While they do this, they leave behind their various properties depending on what they are made of. In this triple Rose flower smudge stick, I have used White Rose petals, because they offer protection and deep purification, and Pink Rose petals, which will lend a graceful energy to a space and help with healing. The addition of Rosemary also offers protection as well as lifting psychic awareness and clarity.

Timings

Waning Moon, Saturday, Midnight

Find and Gather

» Rosemary *(Rosemarinus officinalis)*, preferably in flower
» 1 White Rose *(Rosa)*
» 1 Pink Rose *(Rosa)*
» cotton or hemp string

The Spell

Bunch together about 6–8 large fresh sprigs of Rosemary. Cut a piece of string at least four times the length of your bundle of Rosemary and tie your sprigs together very tightly at one end.

Loosen all the petals off both Roses.

As you wind your string in a spiral type pattern to the end of the bundle of Rosemary, place your Rose petals under the string, against the Rosemary, to anchor them. You want to cover the Rosemary with the Rose petals, but they don't have to cover it completely.

Tie off at the end and cut off the string.

Tie the string again at the bottom and wind the string up the bundle, but this time crossing the previous string at an opposite angle. Again, lay the petals against the bundle and anchor with the string as you go. Make sure you end up with roughly an equal amount of pink and white petals on the bundle firmly held together in the string.

As you are anchoring the Rose petals say:

Triple Rose bundle, protection entwined,
Cleanse and release in the places you find.

Hang your smudge stick in a cool dry place to dry out completely. This could take up to two weeks. To use, carefully light and once it has 'caught', blow out to allow your smudge stick to smoulder. Use a large leaf to fan the smoke around the area you wish to cleanse and protect. Remember to start in the middle of your rooms and work your way out. Have windows and doors all open so that the smoke takes the negativity out with it.

Alternative Flowers

Any flowers that are safe to inhale when burning.

Many plants have the word 'officinalis' in their name, like the Rosemary suggested here. It means that the plant is an important herbal remedy.

To maintain youth, it has been suggested to bath daily in Rosemary water or sniff it daily.

Snapdragon Hex-Breaker Spell

*This powerful hex-breaker relies on the energies of Snapdragon, a plant
I grow and harvest every year in my own garden because it is the most
reliable flower for such magick workings. Snapdragons break all types of
hexes and curses and they do so gracefully and precisely.*

*You will be creating a small and very simple doll that is going to return
the hex to the person who sent it to you.*

Timings
Waning Moon, Wednesday, Midnight

Find and Gather

» a few tablespoons of dried Snapdragon
flowers *(Antirrhinum majus)*

» 2 pieces of red fabric, 15 x 15 cm (6 x 6")

» sewing pins

» 2 tiny safety pins

» a needle

» red thread

» scissors

» black felt-tip pen

» biro and paper

» a postage stamp

The Spell

Pin your fabric pieces together at their centre.

With the felt-tip pen, draw a simple person shape onto the fabric (around the pins). Cut out the shape of the person.

Sew the pieces together along the person shape, leaving a small opening at the top of the head. Fill the doll with Snapdragon flowers and say:

Snapping Dragons all, take this hex far away.
Break it in pieces and lose it today.

Sew up the opening.

With your biro write 'return to sender' on the piece of paper. Pin the paper to front of doll with one small safety pin. With the other safety pin add the postage stamp to the doll.

Take the doll to a place as far away from your home as possible and throw in a bin.

Return home, but not directly. Take your time and take what you would think is a confusing route.

Alternate Flowers

There are no alternatives for this spell.

Need to quickly break a spell? Try stepping on a Snapdragon flower.

In Dutch folklore it is believed that if you want to make your love rivals disappear, then plant a large bed of Snapdragons.

Lilac Space-Clearing Spell

Lilacs are the perfect flowers for a space-clearing spell because they help you remove energies you don't want. They will impart a new and positive vitality to a space and they will assist those connected with the space to move forward with safety, free from any hurtful or negative occurrences or feelings.

Timings
Waning Moon, Saturday, Midnight/Midday

Find and Gather

» Lilac flowers *(Syringa vulgaris)*
» a large white pillar candle
» an additional white taper candle
» a metal spoon
» wax paper

The Spell
Dry your flowers as flat as possible. Pressing would be best.

Lay out your wax paper to protect your work area. Light your taper candle and drip wax onto the side of your pillar candle. Now very quickly press your flowers into the melted wax on your pillar candle. Work in small areas, building up your design.

As you add each flower, say:

Lilac will call you and take you away.

Space to be cleared

When lit from this day.

Once you are happy with the result, drip more taper wax to cover your flowers to seal. You can use the metal spoon to gently spread and push down the wax.

When the wax is dry you can light the candle at any time in the area you wish to energetically clear.

Alternate Flowers

Lemon Blossom *(Citrus limon)*

Lilac's botanical name, 'Syringa', comes to us from the Greek word for 'pipe'. The stem of the flower looks like a pipe and there are references to lilac being the plant that the 'Pipes of Pan' were formed from.

In Wales it is believed that if someone kills or pulls out an entire Lilac bush, the others in the area will not flower the following year in mourning for the lost plant.

Sweet Violet Deception Protection Spell

You will need to make very sure that the Violets you obtain for this spell are both organic and edible – some types are not. This is magickal cooking, so make sure your kitchen is clean and tidy and energetically clear. Also make sure you create with a magickal heart and mind on the task. These deception protection drops can be added to any drink, hot or cold, or as an additional garnish to foods as well.

Timings
Full Moon, Saturday, Late Night

Find and Gather

» 2 dozen organic, edible Sweet Violets *(Viola odorata)*
» 1 cup of regular sugar
» ¼ cup of water
» ½ cup of castor sugar/super fine sugar
» baking paper
» flat baking tray
» tweezers
» flat bowl
» sweet/candy thermometer (optional)
» a small airtight container

The Spell

Place 1 cup of regular sugar and water into a saucepan over a low heat and stir continuously until the liquid begins to boil. Cease stirring and wait until mixture reaches 38°C/100°F or has become reduced to a clear syrup. You can use your thermometer to test the temperature.

Turn off the heat and let cool. Line your tray with the baking paper. Place your castor sugar in a flat bowl. Using your tweezers, dip each violet into the sugar syrup and then sprinkle castor sugar liberally over the flower. Shake off excess and place back on baking tray.

After all are done, say:

Crystal sweet sugar,
From deception protect
Each lovely flower
As they magickally set.

Leave to dry for at least 24 hours and then store in a cool dry place in an airtight container. Use these little flower drops in teas or other drinks when you want to protect yourself from deception.

Alternate Flowers

Other types of edible violets.

Violets were the favourite flower of Empress Josephine. Napoleon planted them on her grave. When he died he was found to have a locket containing a lock of Josephine's hair and a Violet.

In Ancient Greece people wore circlets of Violets to alleviate headaches and to induce a peaceful and deep sleep.

Red Clover Travel Protection Spell

This is, without fail, the very best travel-protection spell I have. Rinsing your hair in this special magick mixture will help to keep you safe on travels near and far. Red clover is able to protect on a multitude of levels as well as bringing good luck. Rosemary is added for its powers to increase psychic awareness and White Rose petals provide protective energies as well as the ability to help people see the truth and remain honest.

Timings
Full Moon, Saturday, Daytime

Find and Gather
» 1 cup of organic Red Clover flowers *(Trifolium pratense)*
» 1 cup of organic White Rose *(Rosa)* petals
» ¼ cup of organic fresh Rosemary *(Rosmarinus officinalis)* with flowers, if possible
» 2½ cups of water and a small pot
» ½ cup of apple cider vinegar
» ¼ cup of olive oil (if you have dry hair)
» a sterilised jar, to store

The Spell

Bring the water to a boil in the pot and then remove from the heat.

Gently stir in the Clover flowers, Rose petals and Rosemary and leave overnight.

Before you leave your brew say:

Sleep pretty flowers,
This night may your powers fill the water.

The next day, strain mixture into the jar and add apple cider vinegar.

Store in the fridge.

To use: Shake the bottle.

After washing your hair, massage 2 tablespoons of the travel-protection hair rinse through your hair and simply say:

Flower water protect me wherever I wander.

You can wash the rinse out or leave it in. You can take the rinse with you on your travels – it will keep for a couple of weeks outside the fridge.

Alternate Flowers

Although there are many flowers that you could use to create a hair rinse, this particular magickal rinse works best with Red Clover flowers as the base.

Adding Red Clover to your bath the day before you need to attend to financial dealings and negotiations will help outcomes go your way.

Red Clover is one of the world's oldest crops and is used primarily as animal fodder. It was also the model for the suit of Clubs in playing cards.

Azalea and Chrysanthemum Personal Protection Spell

Azaleas can assist in self-care and help you stay true to yourself. Azaleas will make sure you do not let negative energies into your personal sphere. Yellow Chrysanthemums are excellent boundary protectors.

This spell is another type of spell bottle like the one prescribed earlier in this book in the Carnation Decision-Making Spell Bottle. You can obtain tiny corked bottles easily from craft stores and online. Some come with pendant fittings already attached should you wish to wear your bottle. Be aware that Azaleas are highly toxic if consumed.

Timings
Full Moon, Saturday, Dusk

Find and Gather
» a dark-coloured Azalea flower (*Rhododendron*)
» a Yellow Chrysanthemum (*Chrysanthemum*)
» a tiny glass corked bottle you can carry with you
» water
» glycerin
» sealing wax
» a piece of black flannel or thick soft cloth to wrap the bottle in
» a thin black ribbon

The Spell

Dry the Azalea and Chrysanthemum flowers using one of the methods mentioned earlier in this book. You will only need a petal from each for this spell.

Crush your petals and add to the glass bottle. Fill the bottle half way at most and say:

Flower of dark,
Flower of light,
Bind together now
and make all things right.

Add a few drops of glycerin and then fill the rest of the bottle with water.

Seal by adding the cork and dipping the entire top in sealing wax.

To store, wrap in a black cloth and tie the thin black ribbon around it.

Whenever you need added personal protection, carry your personal protection spell bottle with you. To keep it safe in a bag or pocket you can leave cloth and ribbon on. When you need to add an extra boost to your personal space, shake the bottle and repeat the chant above.

Alternate Flowers

Azalea » Lily *(Lilium)*, Yellow Chrysanthemum » Red Clover *(Trifolium pratense)*

It is thought that if you wear Chrysanthemums you will be protected from the wrath of the Gods.

Honey created from the nectar of Azaleas is known as 'mad honey' and usually causes confusion, vomiting, convulsions, and ultimately, death.

Cornflower Home Protection Spell

Cornflowers can provide a natural dye and we are going to use this attribute to create a little flag to hang at your front door to offer you protection. You may wish make bunting or a larger flag. This mixture should dye up to about a shirt's worth of fabric. If you wish to dye more fabric, adjust the measurements accordingly.

·

Timings

Full Moon, Monday, Evening

Find and Gather

» 2 cups of fresh, finely chopped Cornflowers
   (*Centaurea cyanus*)

» a 30x30 cm (12x12") piece of natural fabric
   (cotton, silk, linen)

» 4 cups of cold water

» 1 cup of white vinegar

» a bowl for this purpose only

» a glass or stainless-steel pot for this purpose only

» 4 cups of room-temperature water

» protective covering for work areas (plastic sheet is best)

» gloves

The Spell

Before beginning to chop your Cornflowers, say:

Powerful flowers of protection and knowledge
I thank you for sharing your wisdom and care.

Wash fabric, rinse very well and leave damp.

Mix together 4 cups of cold water and vinegar in your bowl and add fabric. Leave for an hour.

Add Cornflowers to the stainless-steel pot and add 4 cups of room-temperature water and then simmer for at least an hour until you obtain the colour you desire.

Put on your gloves. Strain the coloured water back into the bowl, discarding flowers as you do so (bury in the garden near your front door). Be careful with straining as this mixture will dye anything it touches. You may wish to purchase a cheap strainer just for this purpose, or use a piece of cheesecloth.

Return liquid to the pot. Put on the heat again and add the fabric. Simmer for another hour and turn off the heat. Leave fabric in this mixture until it is the depth of colour you would like.

When happy, take out the cloth and rinse really well.

Cut into a flag shape, hem the edges, hang near your front door and say three times:

All within are safe,
Under the flag of Cornflower grace.

Alternate Flowers

There are no alternatives for this particular spell.

The botanical name of Cornflower is 'Centaurea' and refers to Chiron, the centaur who Achilles gained herbal medical skills from.

Cornflowers are also known as 'Bachelor's Buttons'. Men would wear them to indicate they were available and interested in courtship.

Lemon Blossom Freeze-and-Banish Spell

Lemon Blossom is a wonderful flower to call on when you need to remove something from your life. Not only are these flowers very good at clearing unwanted energies, they are wonderful deep space clearers and they banish negativity completely.

Timings
Waning Moon, Tuesday, Midnight

Find and Gather
» 3 Lemon Blossom *(Citrus limon)* flowers
» pure water
» a small plastic container
» a small piece of paper
» a pen

The Spell
Sit and write down on your paper the thing that you want removed from your life.

Fold the paper, place it in your plastic container and say:

In you go,
Your energy flows.

Place the three Lemon Blossoms on top of the paper and say:

One for cleansing,
Your light now fades.
One for closing,
Your memory done.
One for leaving me,
Your power now gone.

Now pour the water to fill the container and place in the freezer. As you do, say:

Frozen you are,

No longer you move.

Be gone from my life,

And never return.

Alternate Flowers

Any Citrus Blossom.

Lemon juice diluted in water is an excellent purifier of magickal tools. Be careful you only use a little as it does have bleaching properties. Eating lemons also increases your psychic and magickal powers.

We now know, thanks to DNA, that lemons are most likely to be a hybrid of Bitter Orange (Citrus aurantium) and Citron (Citrus medica).

Heather Danger-Shielding Spell

Heather flowers, both lavender-coloured and white, hold valuable properties that assist in the creation of this blessing water. You can use this water to cleanse magickal objects, and to impart protection blessing upon objects and also people.

White Heather can protect from danger and grant wishes, courage and faith.

Lavender Heather assists with the removal of negative energies, instills good luck and can also assist those seeking a peaceful sleep if suffering nightmares.

Timings
Full Moon, Sunday, Night

Find and Gather
» a handful of White Heather (*Calluna vulgaris*)
» a handful Lavender Heather (*Calluna vulgaris*)
» a large pinch of salt
» 3 drops of rose essential oil
» a white candle
» 1 cup of pure water
» a glass/crystal bowl
» a glass misting bottle

The Spell

Make sure that you work under the light of the Moon.

Light your white candle.

Pour your pure water and rose essential oil into your bowl and say:

Water of crystal light,

May the light of candle and moon bless you.

Sprinkle in salt over the water and say:

Salt of the earth,

Balance and ground.

Add your Lavender Heather flowers and say:

Heather flowers,

Remove all the darkness you find.

Add your White Heather and say:

Heather flowers,

Protect all the light you find.

Bottle your water in your misting bottle.

Blow out your candle and say:

I thank light for the blessings.

Alternate Flowers

Roses of different colours are suitable, White Rose *(Rosa)* in particular.

Heather stalks provide food for faeries. If you find a field of Heather, you may very well stumble upon a faerie portal to their world.

It is said in English folklore that you can make it rain by burning Heather and a Fern sprig together outdoors.

Lavender Ultimate Protection Spell

This weaving spell is best used when you know exactly what you need
protection from. It is a weaving spell and you will need rather long
stalks of lavender in order to achieve a good result. French lavender is
best. Lavender also cleanses. The inherent qualities of grace and trust in
Lavender also assist in strengthening your spell vessel, and the energies
you weave into it. Make sure you are completely focussed on this task.

Timings
Waning Moon, Saturday, Midday

Find and Gather
» 33 long stems of fresh Lavender *(Lavandula)*
» 200 cm/90" of lavender-coloured ribbon
» scissors

The Spell
Carefully strip all the foliage from each stem from below the flower head. You
can do this by slowly pulling it off in a downward motion.

Hold the bunch together and tie one end of the ribbon firmly under the
flowers to keep them together.

Turn the bunch upside down and then fold each stem back over the bunch
of flowers.

Begin weaving the ribbon through the bent stems, up and over each stem to ensure a checkerboard pattern emerges. Keep your weaving firm so that you are enclosing the flowers within.

While you are weaving, say:

Over and under,

Above and below,

Weaving protection

Wherever I go.

Once you have woven enough to encase the flowers, keep going a little more to neaten up, pulling the weaving tight to completely enclose the flowers. Then tie off with a knot and bow at the top of the bundle around all of the stems.

This spell vessel can be hung in an area you would like to protect, or shake it three times before you set out to do whatever it is that you are seeking additional protection for.

Alternate Flowers

There are no alternatives for this spell.

Lavender is thought to be a very attractive scent to men and so has a long history as an aphrodisiac. Cleopatra wore it as a perfume, Victorian woman bathed in Lavender water before meeting their love interests, and in England it was an extremely popular bed linen scent for centuries.

Carrying or wearing Lavender will avert the evil eye.

FLOWER SPELLS
for HEALTH
and HEALING

Peony Vitality and Good Health Spell

This spell involves creating a classic Pot Pourri using a traditional method. It is particularly good for times when you are seeking physical immunity or recuperating from illness. It does take about two months to create, so make it as flowers are in season and store for use throughout the year. Peony and Pink Roses are the main flowers in this Pot Pourri spell because of their strong healing powers. The addition of Marigold imparts strength and vitality.

Timings
Full Moon, Thursday, Midday

Find and Gather
» 1 cup of Peony *(Paeonia officinalis)* petals

» 3 cups of Pink Rose *(Rosa)* petals

» 1 cup of Marigold *(Tagetes evecta)* petals

» 1 cup of Rose leaves

» ¼ cup of orris root powder

» 3 drops of Rose essential oil

» 3 drops of lemon oil

» 3 cups of cooking salt

» a large airtight container and lid

» a beautiful, open bowl or container

Paeonia Montan

- » a pink cloth
- » a peridot stone

The Spell

Mix all of your fresh flower petals together. Place a layer into your airtight container and then sprinkle with a layer of the salt.

Keep layering fresh flowers and salt until you use up all your flowers and finish off with a layer of salt. Seal and wrap the container in pink cloth and store in a cool, dry place for two weeks.

After two weeks, open and break up the hardened mixture and mix in the essential oils and orris root powder and the peridot. Place back into container, seal and wrap in pink cloth again, and leave in a cool, dry place for six weeks.

To use, place into a beautiful bowl and leave in places near to you to impart the healing and strengthening energy of these flowers.

You can refresh the fragrance and boost the energy of the mix by adding a few drops of essential oils from time to time.

Alternate Flowers

Peony » a cup of Pink Rose Petals *(Rosa)*

Marigold » Sunflower *(Helianthus annuus)*

Peony is named after Paeon, who studied the usage of plants for healing, and who was a student of Aesculapius, the Greek god of medicine.

Peony roots were once carved to create 'piney beads'. These beads formed a necklace that would protect the wearer from faeries and evil.

Elderflower Rejuvenation Spell

This spell involves the creation of a rejuvenating beauty oil, which is not only beneficial for your skin but also boosts confidence, lifts negative attitudes, boosts self-esteem and helps promote vigour and resilience via the Elderflower.

Timings
Full Moon, Sunday, Morning

Find and Gather
» 1 cup of Elderflowers *(Sambucus nigra)*
» 1 cup of Chamomile flowers (*Matricaria retutica)*
» 1 cup of Rose *(Rosa)* petals
» ½ cup of almond oil
» ½ cup of apricot oil
» ½ cup of avocado oil
» ¼ cup of rosehip oil
» ¼ cup of olive oil
» 1 teaspoon of vitamin E oil
» muslin cloth
» large sealable glass jar
» sterilised jar/s to keep

- » yellow cloth, large enough to wrap around your jar
- » yellow ribbon, approximately 30cm (12") in length
- » Rose essential oil

The Spell

Add the flowers and the oils (except the Rose essential oil) to the large glass jar and say:

Flowers gather together and rest in the oil.

Now is your time to rest for a while.

Seal the jar and wrap in yellow cloth and keep in a warm place. Every morning for nine days knock on the jar gently and say:

Wake up, wake up now flowers and oil.

On the ninth day strain the oil through muslin cloth, into sterilised jar/s to store. Add as much Rose essential oil as you like to each mix. Go lightly at first – you can always add more at a later time. Tie a yellow ribbon around the neck of the jar. Store in the fridge and bury the strained flowers in a sunlit area. Do a patch test of the oil first by putting a small dab on your inner arm for 48 hours.

To experience the rejuvenating magick of this oil, each morning place a few dabs on your face and massage in. As you do, say:

Renewed and refreshed, in body and mind.

Alternate Flowers

Any flower that is safe for topical use can be substituted except Elder Flower.

In Russian folklore, placing Elderflower branches around windows and doorways protects against vampires and the devil, who would be too busy counting the blossoms or berries.

Sunflower Strength and Courage Spell

Bring the strength of sunshine in to help speed up recuperation. Marigold imparts vitality and vigour, and supports renewal as well as having strong connections with life-force energies. Sunflower is a physical healer and supports strength and courage.

Timings

Full Moon, Sunday, Midday

Find and Gather

» a Sunflower *(Helianthus annuus)*

» a few Marigolds *(Tagetes evecta)*

» wax paper, 30 x 30 cm (12" x 12")

» newspaper

» washi or pretty masking tape

» an electric iron

» golden ribbon, long enough to hang your suncatcher with

The Spell

Pluck the petals from your flowers and dry thoroughly according to the directions at the beginning of this book. It would be preferable to use a method that presses them.

You can make these suncatchers in any size and use any number; in fact, a collection hanging in the window of someone facing health challenges would not only be helpful, but rather beautiful.

Cut your wax paper into two identical shapes. You may like to start with circles but any shape including diamonds, triangles, squares would be suitable.

Lay one piece on wax paper on some newspaper. Arrange your Sunflower and Marigold petals on the wax paper in patterns that please you. Recreating the symbol of the sun or a star is very helpful for this spell.

Lay the other piece of wax paper on top and lay a piece of newspaper over the lot.

Using your iron on a medium heat, press your creation carefully until the wax melts and fuses the wax papers together.

As you press, say:

Flowers of sun, may you shine health, courage and strength over all.

Finish off the edges with your washi/decorative tape or you may like to sew a decorative edge around your suncatcher. Hang in windows to catch the sunlight, empower the flowers within. Share with everyone who is near.

Alternate Flowers

There are no alternatives for this spell.

Sunflowers (Heliathus annuus) are native to the Americas, so most references to 'Sunflowers' throughout the rest of the world, in literature and folklore prior to external discovery of these countries, refer to Marigolds and other flowers which appear to track the sun. If you wish to know the truth about something, sleep with a single Sunflower seed under your bed. The truth will be revealed within a week.

Dahlia Detox Spell

These drops help those who are undergoing a detox or experiencing a withdrawal from something. The drops are created with the help of Dahlia flowers, which impart incredibly supportive energy: they boost inner strength and confidence; instill greater faith and resiliency while constantly encouraging.

Timings
Waning Moon, Thursday, Midday

Find and Gather
» a Dahlia flower *(Dahlia)*
» pure water
» a glass/crystal bowl
» a glass storage bottle
» small dropper bottles (optional)

The Spell
You will be creating a flower essence in this spell, so you will need a sunny day with preferably an hour of clear sunlight.

Set your bowl up in the sunlight in a place where it will be safe.

Pour your water into the bowl and say:

Pure water, ready to hold the energy of Dahlia.

Encouragement, confidence, vitality, inner strength, faith and resiliency keep.

Place your Dahlia flower upon the water and say:

Stay a while and leave behind,

The gifts I seek, flower beautiful and wise.

Sit with your flower spell for exactly an hour. Do not touch it or move it.

Relax and focus on your commitment to your detox. After the hour, remove the flower and thank it. Place it in the shade of a tree.

Pour the water into the storage bottle. You can also pour into smaller dropper bottles to carry around with you. The water will keep in the fridge for a month, but if you wish to extend its life and store it outside refrigeration, add 1 part glycerin to 4 parts flower-essence water.

To use, add three drops to a glass of water three times a day, and drink.

Alternate Flowers

Pink Carnation *(Dianthus caryophyllus)*

Dahlia, which originated in Mexico, was cultivated and prized by the Aztecs for its various medicinal properties.

Empress Josephine adored Dahlias and had an impressive collection in her gardens. She loved to think she was the only person in Europe to grow them; so when some were stolen, she had the rest destroyed. Being tubers, however, they grew back.

Hibiscus Stress Release Spell

This spell creates a beautiful, calming magickal lip balm, which not only ensures calmness and stress relief, but will give you lovely soft lips. By using as a lip balm, what you say and do as you go about your day will not be tainted with any stress you have had to endure.

Hibiscus is used as the primary flower in this spell due to its ability to connect us to happiness and instill a stronger belief in our abilities.

Timings
Waning Moon, Saturday, Midday

Find and Gather

» ½ cup of organic Hibiscus flower petals
   (Hibiscus)
» 3 drops of lavender essential oil
» 1 cup of organic olive oil
» 2 tablespoons of vitamin E oil
» 1 tablespoon of honey
» 40 gms/1.5oz beeswax
» small, sterilised containers to keep lip balm in

The Spell

Over a low heat, slowly warm the hibiscus flower petals in the oil for 30 minutes and say:

Hibiscus lovely,

happy and true,

When next I wear

Let me be more like you.

Strain oil, discard petals by burying in garden and then return oil to very low heat.

Stir in vitamin E oil, honey and beeswax and keep stirring until beeswax has melted.

Remove from heat and beat until mixture is smooth.

As you are whipping your lip balm, say:

Air take all thoughts,

Tainted, tangled and heavy.

Pour into containers and allow to cool before use.

Alternate Flowers

Pink or White Roses (*Rosa*)

In many nations the Hibiscus is known as the Queen of the Tropics as well as a symbol of happiness and peace.

A popular thirst-quenching herbal iced tea known as 'karkade' is created from Red Hibiscus, in North Africa. Thought to be an aphrodisiac, women are often prohibited from drinking it.

Moonflower Stop Nightmares Spell

This is not the easiest flower to obtain, but because this spell uses the imagery of Moonflower, an image on an oracle card, artwork or photo which you are really drawn to will do.

There are many plants that share the common name of Moonflower, but all look over the dream state and ensure peaceful dreams as well as increasing power over negative dreams.

Timings

Waning, Saturday, Evening

Find and Gather

- » 1 Moonflower *(Ipomoea alba)* or an image of one
- » a small easel or frame
- » pens/pencils
- » sketch pad
- » silver paint
- » small paint brush
- » 2 blue candles
- » a white cloth
- » a candlesnuffer

The Spell

Lay out your white cloth on your nightstand or a surface close to your bed. Place your candles in candleholders on either side of the cloth. Place your Moonflower/oracle card or image in frame or on easel between the two candles.

Light the candles and say:

Light fills the dark,
With your brilliant clean spark.
Moonflower of power
Hold the light with your flower.

Sit before your Moonflower or Moonflower image and draw your flower. This is not an art test and the artistic merit is not important at all; in fact, it will be more powerful if you draw your flower without looking at the paper. Gaze at the Moonflower and focus on its line and shape. When you have finished, take the silver paint and paintbrush and lightly colour your creation. When completed, say:

Silver healing light, take hold of my flower.
Bring healing light while shielding my dreams from negativity.

Place your picture in place of the Moonflower or oracle card/image and snuff the candles out.

Leave your image and spell for a few nights. Relight the candles for a while each night until they have burnt down.

Alternate Flowers

There are no alternatives for this spell.

The Moonflower's fragrance is beautiful, but not all of us can smell it – you need to have a certain gene to detect the scent.

Morning Glory Habit-Breaker Spell

Grids help focus energy and hold it for a period of time. Grids are therefore very helpful in spells that provide you with a little more time. Habits are usually formed over time and so it makes sense to use magick that is of a longer duration to ensure they are broken completely.

Using Morning-Glory as a habit breaker supports commitment to change. As each day dawns, these flowers impart vitality, which can help with personal energies as you go through withdrawal from any habit.

Timings
· Waning, Saturday, Early Morning

Find and Gather
- » 4 Morning-Glory flowers (*Ipomoea purpurea*)
- » 4 small vases
- » pure water
- » a flat stone
- » 4 white feathers
- » black fine marker

The Spell
Find a place where you can set up this spell and leave it for up to a week or more.

The space should be big enough to contain your spell grid as described below and not be disturbed.

On your flat stone write down what the habit is that you wish to break.

Place it in the centre of your space and say:

Lay here habit, you are not going to leave.

Your power over me will break this week.

Place each vase around the stone. Add water to the vases and say:

Pure sweet water, life you sustain.

But only good things from now on remain.

Add a Morning-Glory flower to each vase and say:

This is the last morning my habit will hold.

Flowers of dawn take it away.

Between each vase, in a pattern, place a white feather and say:

Light as the breeze, fly my habit away.

Never return, not even a day.

Stand back and say:

A flower grid with feather and stone.

Once the blooms have left, habit leave me alone.

Your habit will be broken once the flowers are spent. Once they are spent, take them, the feathers and stone to a place far away from your home and bury in a dark place. Return home in a non-direct route so your habit won't follow you.

Alternate Flowers

Common Thistle (Cirsium vulgare)

Although it is considered a noxious weed in many countries, if Morning-Glory grows well in your garden, peace and happiness is assured.

Morning-Glory flowers were used by the Aztecs and other South American peoples as a way to communicate with the gods.

White Chrysanthemum Health Commitment Spell

White Chrysanthemums help you stay committed to promises made. In this spell you will be creating a rather lovely mirror to help you stay committed to a promise made each day.

Timings
Full Moon, Wednesday, Morning

Find and Gather

» a bunch of dried White Chrysanthemums *(Chrysanthemum)* with stems of at least 6 cm/2.5"
» a mirror with a flat, plain frame
» raffia
» glue gun
» wire
» pen and paper

The Spell
Write out a list of things you could do to improve your health.

Raffia Plait Frame: Work out how thick you would like your plait to be. You may like it as thick as the mirror frame, or thinner. Lay out your raffia in a thickness to suit. Neatly wrap 15 cm/6" of wire around one end of the raffia, to secure it. Divide the raffia into three equal sections and plait. Keep going until you have a length that will go right around your mirror. Bind the end as you did the beginning. If your raffia runs out before the length you need is achieved, simply make more plaits until you have enough. As you plait, envision yourself as healthy as possible and what you might need to do to achieve that health. Picture yourself happily eating, living and thinking positively. Any time a negative thought comes into your head, say:

Over and under, through darkness and light,
Healthy and happy, with all of my might.

Using the glue gun, attach your plaits to your mirror so that they frame it. This is the most secure way of affixing your raffia to a flat surface. But for the sake of magick, never use such a method for securing your flowers.

Hang your mirror in a place where you will see it first thing in the morning. Stand before your mirror and thread your White Chrysanthemums into the plait frame.

With each flower set in the plait, read out a different commitment you will make to ensure better health. Extra flowers can be saved and added at later date for additional commitments or re-commitments you wish to add.

Each day look into the mirror and say:

I remain committed today to each flower I see.

Alternate Flowers

There are no alternatives for this spell.

Originating in China, Chrysanthemums were noted by Confucius in his writings 500 years before the birth of Christ.

Drinking from a glass with a single Chrysanthemum petal in the bottom will ensure health and longevity.

Madonna Lily and Pink Rose Healing Spell

Together, Madonna Lily and Pink Rose form a powerful bond perfect for healing. Madonna Lily will also help to uncover reasons for illness, pathways for recovery, protection, and encouragement to heal. Pink Roses offer strong healing energies and stand by as a friend to offer support.

Timings

Full Moon, Thursday, Midnight

Find and Gather

» a Madonna Lily *(Lilium candidum)*
» a Pink Rosa *(Rosa)*
» either a piece of rose quartz crystal or rose quartz set in a piece of jewellery
» a pink candle
» a darning needle, awl or blunt pen to inscribe the candle
» a glass or crystal bowl
» pure water

The Spell

Pour water into your bowl until it is half full.

Add your pink quartz crystal or jewellery to the water and say:

Cleanse in the water,

Clear and clear.

Place your Madonna Lily in the water and say:

Lady of flowers, show me the way.

Protect and encourage me each of my days.

Place your Pink Rose in the water and say:

Rose of great friendship,

Stand with me here with your comfort and cheer.

Take your candle and inscribe a spiral sun. This will look like a small spiral circle with rays coming out around it to look like a sun. This symbol is one that will encourage healing.

Light the candle so that the reflection of the flame is caught in the water.

Let the candle burn down while you attend it. Take out your crystal/jewellery.

It is now ready to carry or wear as a powerful healing tool.

Dry the flowers and add to a small bag and carry with you should you wish to boost healing.

Alternate Flowers

Madonna Lily » other White Lily *(Lilum)*

Pink Rose » White Rose *(Rosa)*

The Ancient Greeks associated Lily with Hera, the goddess of home, motherhood and marriage. In Rome, a similar goddess, Juno, represented these qualities.

It is said in many folklores that Lilies will always grow best for a good woman and, in some instances, fail completely if she has been in any way dishonest.

Everlasting Daisy Immunity Spell

This spell involves creating a pillow sachet, which can be added to an everyday pillow or cushion slip. You could make this pillow any size you like, however, and not attach it to another pillow at all. Smaller pillows make wonderful gifts for others. Fabrics will also add their meanings to your spell crafting. The use of flannel in this spell is to impart the energies of protection and also comfort.

Timings
Waxing, Sunday, Midday

Find and Gather

- » 1 cup of Everlasting Daisies *(Rhodanthe chlorocephala)* or *(Helichrysum)*
- » 1 x 15 cm/6" square piece of beautiful fabric
- » 2 x 15 cm/6" square pieces of soft flannel or similar fabric
- » sewing pins
- » sewing machine or needle and gold thread
- » 3 drops of tea-tree essential oil
- » 3 drops of rosemary essential oil
- » 3 drops of lemon essential oil
- » large glass bowl

The Spell

Dry Everlasting Daisies completely according to instructions at the beginning of this book.

In your bowl, mix dried flowers with essential oils and set aside.

With your needle and gold thread, sew together your piece of beautiful fabric and a piece of flannel. Your beautiful fabric will be on the top of your pillow to ensure it is comfortable against your skin, so make sure you find a fabric that won't scratch you.

Pin your completed pillow to the remaining flannel square and sew together, leaving a small opening.

Fill your pillow with your Everlasting Daisies and take outside into the sunshine. Sitting in the warmth of the sun, try to catch some sunlight in the opening you have left on your pillow and say:

In you go, sunshine.
Stay brilliant and long.
May those who lay upon this pillow
stay healthy and strong.

Then carefully close up the opening by sewing the pillow closed. Sew this onto a pillow or cushion slip or use alone.

Alternate Flowers

Other types of Everlasting Daisies.

Everlasting Daisies are also known as Strawflowers and Paper Daisies. Both Everlasting Daisies are found throughout the world, while Rhodanthe is an Australian Wildflower but a popular international florist flower.

FLOWER SPELLS *for* TRANSITION *and* CHANGE

Gardenia Divination Spell

I love using Gardenia in spells — it has a wonderful way of reaching out and connecting with us and directing us to divine messages. Next time you are drawn to a Gardenia, pay attention to what you are doing and what is around you. One of the aims of this spell is to enrich your spell box with Gardenia's strong powers to receive messages.

Timings

Full Moon, Wednesday, Late Night

Find and Gather

» a dried Gardenia flower *(Gardenia jasminoides)*
» a beautiful wooden box
» a piece of lavender-coloured silk, at least the size of a handkerchief
» 9 small, clear quartz crystals
» a small mirror that will fit in the bottom of the box

The Spell

On the evening of the Full Moon, take your mirror and capture the image of the Full Moon in it. Place your lavender cloth loosely into your box and then place your mirror on top and say:

Light has come, from above to below.

Hold it tight, to help me know.

Place your Gardenia into the box and say:

Listen, flower, day and night.

When I open the box, bring messages to light.

Place the crystals around the Gardenia and, as you add each, say:

Protect and empower.

You can use your divination spell box on its own or to assist you when using other forms of divination such as tarot or oracle cards, runes, pendulum work and so on.

Set the box before you and simply open it and look inside. You may experience certain feelings that will guide you, or hear/see/feel actual messages. Leave open while you are working with divination and then close when complete. You should simply thank your spell box before putting it away.

Alternate Flowers

Gardenia really is the preferred flower but you could use a White Rose *(Rosa)*

Gardenias are members of the coffee family, Rubiaceae. The name Gardenia means 'garden flower'.

Wearing Gardenia either fresh, in artistic form, or in a perfume, will attract new friends and love. It will also ensure that you are protected from the negative influences of others.

Stephanotis Planning Spell

*Stephanotis supports us while we plan, usually major things, in our lives.
This spell works really well for those planning travel, events such as
weddings, and business plans. You will be able to keep this shaker tool to
help 'shake things up' down the track or to make needed adjustments.*

Timings

Waxing Moon, Sunday, Morning

Find and Gather

» a handful of Stephanotis flowers
  (*Stephanotis floribunda*)

» a cardboard tube

» a marker

» an A4 sheet of sturdy cardboard (you can
  recycle a used mailing tube with caps for
  this and the previous two items)

» orange paint

» paintbrush

» a handful of dry rice

» packing tape

» an awl or sharp-pointed tool to make holes in the tube

The Spell

Dry flowers well according ot the instructions at the beginning of this book. Paint your cardboard tube and A4 cardboard sheet with the orange paint. You may wish to be a little more creative and paint a design. Just make sure that the overall colours are oranges, which boost planning energies.

When your tube is completely dry, pierce it a few times all around. Make sure the holes are much smaller than the rice grains.

Stand your cardboard tube upright on your A4 cardboard sheet and trace out two circles. These will serve as the ends of your shaker. Cut both out and, using the packing tape, seal a circle to one end of your cardboard tube. Make sure it is well sealed so your spell doesn't fall out. Now fill your tube with your flowers and rice. Sprinkle in a few drops of the orange essential oil. Seal the tube with the other circle.

To use:

When you are settling down to undertake any activity connected to planning, shake your Stephanotis flower planning shaker and say:

Stir up the energies, come now my way,
For I have decided that today is the day.
Clear all the muddling, untangle the mess,
Planning (insert what you are planning)
and doing my best.

Alternate Flowers

There are no alternative flowers for this spell.

The flower name Stephanotis comes from the Greek word 'stephanos', which means crown, and 'otis', which means ear (the stamens are ear-shaped).

Sacred Blue Water Lily Second-Chance Spell

Tablets with magical symbols, pictures, numbers and words on them have been used since ancient times to import their energy upon all in their space. This tablet will be embedded with Sacred Blue Lily, so will hold the promise of rebirth, second chances and understanding, to repair a relationship, take advantage of an opportunity, or try something again. The size of the tablet is completely up to you but you will find directions below to create a tablet of approximately 10cm/4" x 14cm/5".

Timings
New Moon, Sunday, Morning

Find and Gather

» 2 tablespoons of Sacred Blue Water Lily
   (Nymphaea caerulea), dried
» air-dry clay
» rolling pin
» wax paper/baking paper
» knife
» thick white ribbon
» thin yellow ribbon
» an earth-coloured cloth
» 3 tiny bells

The Spell

Prepare your air-dry clay as per the directions it came with. For the size mentioned below, use a piece roughly the size of your palm. Sprinkle Sacred Blue Water Lily over the clay and then knead it in well. Place on the waxed/baking paper and roll out to 1.5cm/.5" in thickness.

Create a hole in the top, big enough to thread your thick ribbon through. Create eleven smaller holes along the bottom, large enough for the thinner ribbons to thread through. When creating these holes, take into consideration any shrinkage that may occur with your clay.

Place your clay on your earth-coloured cloth and leave to dry. Once completely dry, thread through the thick ribbon, to hang. Tie your yellow ribbons to the bottom of the tablet. Make them long enough so that when the tablet is hanging from a doorway, you can reach up and touch the ribbons as you walk under them. Tie your tiny bells on to some of the ribbons.

Hang the tablet in a doorway and say:

Empowered with chances, tablet of clay,

Hold them close and then release when I say.

Each day as you leave the bedroom or house, reach up and lightly touch your ribbons to make the bells sound.

Alternate Flowers

Bee Balm (*Mondarda*)

Often mistaken for a Lotus, Nymphaea caerulea is also known as Egyptian Lotus. It has been used in perfumery, rituals, and medicinally, since Ancient Egyptian times.

Sacred Blue Water Lily open sky-blue petals to reveal a golden, sun-coloured centre, which represents the Sun god and life itself in Ancient Egypt.

Sweet Alyssum Clarity Spell

Mists can be used to fill spaces around us with magickal energy. In this spell, the properties of Sweet Alyssum flowers, mental release, understanding and clarity, are obtained via a traditional flower essence creation method. This mixture is then placed in a misting bottle that can be used where clarity is required.

Timings
New Moon, Sunday, Morning

Find and Gather

» 11 Sweet Alyssum flowers, preferably white
   (*Lobularia maritime*)
» pure water
» a glass or crystal bowl
» glycerin
» misting bottle

The Spell
Place your glass/crystal bowl on the ground in a sunny spot, which will remain so for at least an hour. Make sure it is on the earth or grass so that it becomes 'grounded'.

Half fill your glass/crystal bowl with the pure water and say:
Water pure, ready to hold,

Flower energy and the power from light gold.

Gently float the Sweet Alyssum flowers upon the water and say:

11 flowers, clear and bright,

Bring me clarity and full, clear sight.

Leave out in the full sun for an hour. Take flowers out and bury with thanks under a large, healthy tree. Bottle the water in misting bottle with 4 parts water to 1 part glycerin. Spray into the space around you when you are seeking clarity.

Alternate Flowers

Boronia (*Boronia ledifolia*), Dandelion *(Taxaxacum officinale)*

To calm someone angry, simply place Sweet Alyssum in their hands or on their body. You could try shaking their hand with some of the flowers in yours.

Sweet Alyssum is well-known as a spell-, hex- and curse-breaker. To ensure protection from any enchantments being cast on you, hang above your bed/ main living area of your home.

Magnolia New Home Search-and-Protect Spell

Magnolia is a flower denoting strength, wisdom and longevity. It is a very supportive flower through times of change, which makes it a really good choice for spells involving the search for a new home.

In this spell we are creating a spell bottle and filling it with items that contain energies that, when shaken together, stir up and release a magickal boost.

When you have found your new home, burying it in the front yard will seal protection for the house and also for those within.

Timings
Waxing, Monday, Evening

Find and Gather
» 1 Magnolia flower *(Magnolia)*
» a beautiful, sealable jar
» 3 bay leaves
» 3 sage leaves
» 1 tablespoon of salt
» 3 cloves of garlic
» 1 tablespoon of black peppercorns
» a small magnifying glass (a child's toy will work)

» a brown ribbon and a blue ribbon

» pure water

» 3 nails

The Spell

Add all your botanicals, except the Magnolia, to the jar and say:

Plants of the land,

A new home seek and find.

Add your Magnolia. You may need to fold it to fit. Then say:

Magnolia sweet and wise, protect and abide.

Fill the jar with your pure water and close the lid. Using both ribbons tie the magnifying glass to the jar. Shake the bottle each morning before you set out to look for your new home and say:

Show me the house, soon to be home.

Once you have found your new home, take the magnifying glass off the bottle. Open the jar and place the three nails inside it. These will 'nail' protection to your home. Bury the jar in your front yard.

Alternate Flowers

Cornflower *(Centaurea cyanus)*

With fossils of the plant dating back over 95 million years, Magnolias are one of the oldest flowers, still in their original form, in existence.

Magnolias have been used in Chinese medicine for centuries. Currently there are more than two hundred patented Chinese medicine drugs based on the Magnolia plant.

Wild Rose New Beginning Spell

An old tradition to clear away the past and welcome the new is to energetically sweep an area of your home, or your entire home. This broom is created using Wild Rose, which is known to help open up new paths. If your way ahead involves contracts, then this flower offers protection for your part in them and assures promises are kept. Lavender also ensures trusts are kept and that you can find a way ahead whilst under protection; it also cleans away anything from the past that may hinder your progress to move forward.

You do not have to create a full-sized broom – the energy will still be the same with a smaller broom as long as it is created in the same manner.

Timings
Waxing Moon, Saturday, Morning

Find and Gather
» Wild Rose (*Rosa acicularis*) with long stems
» Lavender (*Lavandula stoechas*) with long stems
» a small branch to use as a broom handle
» finer sticks to form a brush head
» thick white ribbon
» thinner white ribbon

The Spell

Go for a walk and find a suitable small branch/stick and some smaller sticks to create your broom. Thank the area where you found your gifts.

Using your thick white ribbon, tie your smaller sticks around your large branch to form a broom.

Tie your flowers into the broom by threading them into the sticks and tying with the thinner white ribbon. The flowers can be fresh or dried. Leave them in the broom and store it in a cool, dry place. Hanging your broom will let the flowers dry out.

To usher in your new beginning:

Holding the broom, start in the middle of your home/office/space and use a sweeping motion. You do not have to touch the ground because you are sweeping the energy.

Move from the centre to the outside, and say:

I am making way for the new to come in.

A new beginning awaits.

Clear away what now impedes,

And leave all the things that I need.

Alternate Flowers

Wild Rose » Lupin *(Lupinus perennis)*

Lavender » no substitution.

It has been discovered that Wild Roses existed more than 35 million years ago.

The buttonhole in men's jacket lapels was always there to hold flowers, usually a Rose. It was thought that men who wore a Rose would be afforded luck with the women they met.

Tuberose Obstacle Remover Spell

This spell involves creating a magickal eraser to release obstacles. Tuberose will assist you in getting what it is you desire. This flower also offers protection and strength, which are important while you are focussed on your goal.

TUBEROSE.

Timings

Waning Moon, Thursday, Dusk

Find and Gather

» 1 single Tuberose flower *(Polianthes tuberosa)*

» a slice of white bread with crusts

» a 6H pencil

» a piece of white paper

» a knife

» a wooden chopping board

» a glass of warm water

The Spell

Write down your obstacle/s as faintly as possible but so you can still read it/them on the piece of white paper.

Place your piece of white bread on your chopping board, with the crusts laying parallel to the cardinal directions. Slice off the North crust and say:

Free to the North.

Repeat for each direction as you slice your crusts away. Chop each crust up finely and scatter over the earth.

Finely chop up one Tuberose flower and then sprinkle it over the crust-less piece of white bread. Start kneading the bread and flower pieces together until you form a putty-like ball. Roll the ball between your palms until it firms up.

Use this ball to erase your obstacles from the paper, and say:

Open the borders,
Let the air flow.
May what I desire,
Be free to now go.

Tear up your paper and your magickal eraser into tiny pieces and mix with water. Pour this over the earth and say:

Free now to roam.

Alternate Flowers

Red Tulip *(Tulipa)*, Althea *(Hibiscus syriacus)*

Traditional Hawaiian brides wear a headdress called a haku, which is made of Tuberose and Pikaki flowers.

Tuberoses have a beautiful fragrance, but this scent also stimulates creativity in the brain and can increase a person's emotions, instilling a feeling of blissful serenity.

Jasmine New Opportunity Spell

Jasmine flowers not only herald spring with their flowers, they share the gifts of abundance, victory and hope, with their energy. This spell requires an egg and I would suggest that you make sure you use the egg, not waste it, to ensure that new opportunities coming to you will also not be wasted.

Timings
Waxing Moon, Sunday, Daytime

Find and Gather
» a sprig of Jasmine *(Jasminum officinale)*
» an egg
» sticky tape
» water

The Spell
Under a very old and healthy tree, dig a hole big enough to bury your egg.

Crack your egg and retain the yolk and white for another use. Be very careful and try to crack your egg so that you have two eggshell halves.

Place your Jasmine into one half of your shell and then close it as best as you can with the other half, sealing together with clear tape, and say:

Sweet flower of abundance,
New chances and success.
Help grow them right here,
In the earth I like best.

Bury your magickal egg in the hole you dug under the tree.

For the next nine nights you must return to the place where you buried your egg and sprinkle a little water on the earth covering it, and say:

Grow my hopes little flower,
Make them see light of day.
I ask you tonight,
Send new opportunities my way.

Alternate Flowers

Delphinium *(Delphinium)*

Jasmine flowers are a powerful aphrodisiac and they have many therapeutic benefits. In herbal medicine, they are reputed to regulate blood sugar, improve digestion, improve blood circulation, boost the immune system and act as a calmative.

The Duke of Tuscany introduced Jasmine to Europe in 1699. He refused to share it with anyone, but his gardener gave a sprig to his girlfriend, who grew it. The gardener and his girlfriend then became rather comfortable from selling the flowers.

Snowdrop Career and Last Change Spell

This spell works well if you are looking for a new job or a change in position or career. Importantly, it makes the change last. Snowdrops help bring new beginnings your way and light up the path to find ways to obtain what you are looking for. Jonquils help us define our desires and attain them.

Timings

Waxing Moon, Thursday, Daytime

Find and Gather

- » 1 Snowdrop *(Galanthus nivalis)*
- » 1 Jonquil *(Narcissus jonquilla)*
- » 2 small magnets
- » 2 small pieces of green felt, 11 x 11 cm
- » glue
- » needle and gold thread
- » pen and paper

The Spell

Divide your paper into two pieces no bigger than 6 cm/2.5" square. On one write down what it is you desire e.g: What the job or position is. This will be your 'desire' paper.

On the other piece of paper, write down how you think you may achieve this e.g: Answering an advertisement, winning a contract. This will be your 'path' paper.

Trim your flowers of most of their stems, leaving about 6cm/2.5". Cut your green felt pieces to roughly 11cm/4" square. Leaving a small space on the top, anchor each flower to a piece of the green felt, using the needle and gold thread, by stitching over the stem. Glue a magnet on each piece of felt, on the opposite side to the flower, making sure that the attracting sides face out so when the two pieces of felt are brought together they stick.

Place your two pieces of paper together and then place your Jonquil behind your 'desire' paper and your Snowdrop behind your 'path' paper so that the magnets stick the papers together. The papers will be caught between the pieces of felt when the magnets connect.

Sew a loop through the papers and felt and hang in a front window of your home, and say:

Attract my desires,
And open the path.
The beginning before me,
A place for my heart.

Alternate Flowers

Snowdrops » Daffodils *(Narcissus pseudonarcissus)*
Jonquils » Red Tulip *(Tulipa)*

To dream of Snowdrops means that it is time to share the secret or news you may be withholding from others.

Is it a Daffodil or Jonquil? An easy way to identify each is to remember that Jonquils display multiple flowers on each stem.

Sweet-Pea Change Spell

Sweet Peas are a comforting flower but they also share good luck, protection, and ensure harmony. White Roses offer purification and protection. In this spell you will be making a flower confetti box, which became popular in larger houses in England in the 19th century. These boxes were given to overnight visitors; each would receive a different-coloured flower petal inside. Sprinkling the petals from their room to where dinner was served would ensure, later on, when retiring or wandering around the great halls at night, they would find their way back to the right bed.

Timings
Full Moon, Sunday, Midday

Find and Gather
» a large bunch of Sweet Pea flowers
  (Lathyrus odoratus)
» 6 White Roses
» 1 teaspoon of earth from a place you feel
  attuned to
» a beautiful box

The Spell
Carefully detach and gather all the flower petals. Dry them completely, then crush them with your fingers until they are small, confetti-like pieces.

Place the petals in the box.

The earth you need should be from a place you feel very connected to; a place where you feel comfortable, safe and welcome.

Add the teaspoon of earth to your box, close the lid and shake gently, making the shape of the infinity symbol, while saying:

Things must change, but I go on.

Things must change but gently I go.

Things must change and I change, too.

Gently I bend but on I go.

When you are at the place of change, take some of your flower confetti with you and sprinkle it in a circle around you. This is will help you feel at ease with the changes going on and support you as you adapt to the new path ahead.

Alternate Flowers

Bee Balm *(Monarda)*, Mayflower *(Epigaea repens)*

Carrying a Sweet Pea in your hand will ensure whoever you speak with will only tell the truth.

Most gardeners have favourite secrets to ensure a wonderful crop of Sweet Peas. You could try soaking the seeds in milk overnight or making sure you sow the seeds before sunrise on St Patrick's Day.

Hydrangea Problem Solving Spell

Dedicating a particular bowl to flower scrying is something you might find very useful. A beautiful flat clay bowl is perfect, but any bowl that you feel an affinity with will work.

Hydrangeas are very good at helping you understand a situation and assisting you to keep going until you find solutions. They are also a flower of great interconnectedness between all energies, so are very helpful for problem solving.

Timings
New Moon, Monday, Late Night

Find and Gather

- » Hydrangea *(Hydrangea)*
- » a beautiful, large flat bowl
- » pure water
- » a clear quartz crystal
- » a violet-coloured cloth
- » pencil and sketch pad

The Spell
Lay your cloth out and set your bowl upon it. Pour the pure water into the bowl, filling it about halfway.

Place your quartz crystal into the centre of the bowl.

Carefully remove the Hydrangea flowers and bracts from their stems until you have a lovely pile. The pink or blue petals are actually bracts. The flowers are the tiny centres.

Sit and focus on your problem. Put your fingers in the water and swirl it around in the shape of infinity and say:

All possibilities to solve my problems come to me now.

Set your pencil and sketch pad up.

Cast flowers upon the moving water a few at a time.

Let the water settle between each addition and check in to see what patterns appear. You may like to jot down notes/sketch the images that the petals create, for later study. Perhaps there are letters or images that may be descriptive and indicate direct answers, or the patterns could be symbolic and lead the way to solutions.

Once you have completed your session, bury your flowers in a sunlit place and pour the water over it.

Alternate Flowers

Any flowers can be used for this spell, but Hydrangea are best.

Never plant a Hydrangea along the walls of your home, especially near the front door, if you are single and wish to one day marry. Doing so ensures a lifetime of being alone.

Hydrangea colours are very susceptible to the PH level of soil. Lower than 6.0 and you will see blue tones. Between 6.0 and 7.0 offers purple, and over 7.0 will have your flowers turning pink.

SECTION THREE

How to create your own flower spells

GLADIOLA

Personal flower spells are incredibly powerful because they are so personal. Creating spells from flowers that have special meanings and memories to you, and ones you feel a strong affinity for, can enhance their energies incredibly.

After experiencing and practising some of the flower spells from my collection you may like to create your own based on the methods I have shown you, or to explore other practices. Just remember to also be respectful, safe and focussed.

The pages in your journal are completely blank, so you can fill them as you wish. Use the information at the beginning of the book (for Timings, Crystals, Colours, and so forth) to assist you in creating your own spells.

MAGICKAL CORRESPONDENCES

You may wish to create a bath, an essence, a tea, a mandala; in fact, anything at all will be in itself an action related to the energy of the spell. Items required for this should be aligned with your outcome. These are usually called *Correspondences* or *Magickal Correspondences*. I would suggest that to expand your knowledge in areas that you do not have experience with, you seek out resources that specialise in the item you are wishing to include such as Astrological, Crystal, Colour and so on.

Plate 16

Dandelion

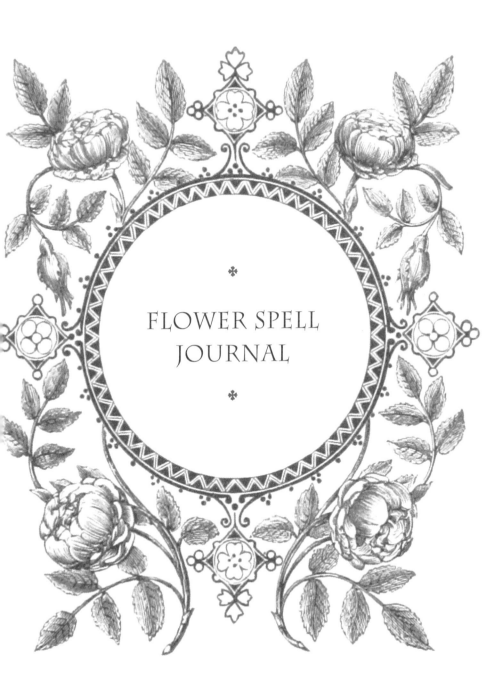

FLOWER SPELL
JOURNAL

Title

....

Description

....

....

....

Find and Gather

....

....

....

The Spell

....

....

....

....

....

....

....

....

....

Title

....

Description

....

....

....

Find and Gather

....

....

....

The Spell

....

....

....

....

....

....

....

....

....

Title

....

Description

....

....

....

Find and Gather

....

....

....

The Spell

....

....

....

....

....

....

....

....

....

Title

....

Description

....

....

....

Find and Gather

....

....

....

The Spell

....

....

....

....

....

....

....

....

....

Title

....

Description

....

....

....

Find and Gather

....

....

....

The Spell

....

....

....

....

....

....

....

....

Title

....

Description

....

....

....

Find and Gather

....

....

....

The Spell

....

....

....

....

....

....

....

....

....

Victoria Aster.
Page 8.

Reid's Quilled Aster.
Page 8.

Dwarf Chrysanthemum Aster.
Page 8.

Flower Meanings

To use a flower in a spell you should understand its energy. To do this, you need to know its meaning. You can discover this by exploring the properties it has or look to resources such as aromatherapy, flower essence guides and flower meaning resources that are based on the language of flowers as well as the actual properties of the plants themselves.

I have included an excerpt from another of my titles, *Flowerpaedia, 1,000 flowers and their meanings*, which shares with you the meanings of some of the flowers in this book. I have sourced these meanings through years of researching the properties of plants.

African Violet *(Saintpaulia)*: spirituality, protection, higher learning

Agapanthus *(Agapanthus praecox)*: love letters, magickal love, my love has not faded, never-fading love

Azalea *(Rhododendron Tsutsusi)*: take care of yourself for me, romance, womanhood, temperance, stay true

Carnation, Red *(Dianthus caryophyllus)*: love, compassion, romance, be mine, abundance, progression, life force, yes

Camellia, Japanese *(Camellia japonica)*: my destiny is in your hands, excellence, concentration, peace, calm

Chrysanthemum, White (*Chrysanthemum*): tell me the truth, trust me, I promise, you are sweet, innocence, purity, honesty

Chrysanthemum, Yellow (*Chrysanthemum*): I cannot be with you, no, refusal, boundary protection

Cornflower (*Centaurea cyanus*): knowledge, protection of home, new friends, friendship, new love, new-home blessings, delicacy

Dahlia (*Dahlia*): you can do this, encouragement, dignity, confidence, vitality, inner strength, creativity, generosity, faith, resilience, instability

Dandelion (*Taraxacum officinale*): I am faithful to you, your wish is granted, long-lasting happiness, healing, intelligence, warmth, power, clarity, survival

Delphinium (*Delphinium*): anything is possible, I have new feelings for you, possibility, new opportunity, protection, new feelings, leadership, communication, true voice

Elder (*Sambucus nigra*): inner strength, self-esteem, courage, fortitude, calm fears, nurturing, stabilise inner energy, vigour, resilience, joy, recovery, renewal of energy, protection from evil, good luck, release sins, prolong life, peaceful sleep

Freesia (*Freesia*): I trust you, life is worthwhile, trust, inner guidance, friendship, innocence, optimism, hope, thoughtfulness

Fuchsia (*Fuchsia magellanica*): true feelings, freeing deep emotions, amiability, confiding love, good taste

Gardenia (*Gardenia jasminoides*): awareness, secret love, divine message

Geranium (*Geranium*): I want to meet you, peace of mind, elegance, comfort, I prefer you, I miss you, fertility, love, virility

Gladiolus (*Gladiolus*): never give up, strength of character, constancy, faith, boundary setting, creative growth, ego

Hibiscus *(Hibiscus)*: you are perfect, delicate beauty, youth, fame, joy, happiness, personal glory

Hydrangea *(Hydrangea)*: you are unfeeling, please understand, perseverance, understanding, interconnectedness, wholeness

Iris, Blue Flag *(Iris versicolor)*: I believe in you, faith, wisdom, valour, purification, spirit messages, creativity, inspiration, ability to be happy, release blocks, eliminate negative feelings

Jasmine *(Jasminum officinale)*: abundance, victory, congratulations, hope

Jonquil *(Narcissus jonquilla)*: returned desire, ease of worry, desire, power, sorrow, death

Lavender *(Lavandula stoechas)*: cleansing, protection, grace, trust, I admire you

Lemon *(Citrus limon)*: I promise to be true, discretion, prudence, fidelity in love, cleansing, space cleansing, banish negative thoughts, zest

Lisianthus *(Eustoma grandiflorum)*: will you marry me? I appreciate you, outgoing nature, appreciation, calming, romantic desire, wedding, gratitude, comfort

Madonna Lily *(Lilium candidum)*: healing, secrets revealed, encouragement, I promise, protection against negativity

Magnolia *(Magnolia campbellii)*: wisdom, acceptance, strength, female energies, changes, I will always love you

Morning Glory *(Ipomoea purpurea)*: habit breaking, consistency, mortality, love in vain, affection, enthusiasm, vitality, love

Nasturtium *(Tropaeolum majus)*: I believe you can succeed, I support you, let's have fun, creative freedom, vitality, fun challenges, independence, over-thinking, jest

Passion Flower *(Passiflora incarnata)*: I am pledged to another, belief, passion, religious superstition, religious work, stability, spiritual balance, higher consciousness

Peony *(Paeonia officinalis)*: I wish you a happy marriage, happy wedding anniversary, wealth, honour, good health, prosperity, romance, compassion, shame, female fertility, nobility

Peruvian Lily *(Alstroemeria)*: I wish you success, I am devoted to you, I am your friend, strength, wealth, good fortune, abundance, prosperity, friendship, devotion

Field Poppy *(Papaver rhoeas)*: memory, continuance, sacrifice, revelations, you are always in my memory

Red Clover *(Trifolium pratense)*: good fortune, good luck, fertility, domestic virtue, protection from danger, psychic protection, cleansing, clear negativity, balance, calmness, clarity, enhance self-awareness

Rose, Red *(Rosa)*: I love you, I respect you, you are beautiful, respect, love, courage, passion, lust, relationship, beauty

Rose, Wild *(Rosa acicularis)*: I trust you, will you marry me?, new path, trust, promises, contracts, betrayal

Rose, Yellow *(Rosa)*: I am your friend, can we be friends? I am falling in love with you, falling in love, welcome back, I will return, friendship, new beginning

Rosemary *(Rosmarinus officinalis)*: I remember you, your presence revives me, psychic awareness, mental strength, accuracy, clarity, remembrance, memory

Sacred Blue Lily *(Nymphaea caerulea)*: rebirth, sacredness, victory, second chance, disconnection, I understand you

Snapdragon *(Antirrhinum majus)*: I'm sorry for what I did, grace under pressure, inner strength, expression of emotions, increased perception, spell breaker, deviousness, grace

Snowdrop *(Galanthus nivalis)*: I am here for you, hope, new beginnings, illumination, inner peace, self neglect, renewal, solutions

Stargazer Lily, Pink *(Lilium orientalis)*: expanded horizons, abundance, spontaneity, wealth, prosperity, ambition

Sunflower *(Helianthus annuus)*: get well, be strong, strength, happiness, male healing, confidence, self-esteem, assertiveness

Sweet Pea *(Lathyrus odoratus)*: you are beautiful, good luck, gratitude, greed, harmony, protection, responsibility, comfort, social responsibility

Sweet Violet *(Viola odorata)*: steadfastness, loyalty, humility, constancy, shyness, protection from deception, protection from inebriation, love potions

Thistle, Scotch *(Onopordum acanthium)*: retaliation, integrity, truth, pride, self-respect

Tuberose *(Polianthes tuberosa):* I desire you, dangerous pleasures, sex, intimacy, protection, strength

Water Lily *(Nymphaea)*: unity, creation, enlightenment, resurrection, purity, gracefulness, separation

Rose jaune de soufre   *Rosa sulfurea*

P.J. Redouté . 62.   Langlois

Glossary

basal: arising from the root crown of a plant

bulb: underground stem with modified leaves that contain stored food for plant shoot within

bract: a modified leaf that sometimes looks like a petal

bracteole: leaf – life projections

cardinal points: directions on a compass

cast: to create and release magick

corm: the underground bulb-like part of some plants

corona: a ring of structures that rise like a tube from a flower

compound: a leaf with a division of two or more small leaf-like structures.

cultivar: a plant that has agricultural and/or horticultural uses and whose unique characteristics are reproduced during propagation

cut flower: a flower used as decoration

dominant hand: the hand you are more proficient with using

endemic: native or restricted to a certain place

flower head: a compact mass of flowers forming what appears to be a single flower

floret: one of the small flowers making up a flower head

Full Moon: when the moon is fully visible as a round disc

grounding: to bring yourself back into the everyday world

hermaphrodite (n): having both male and female reproductive parts

hermaphroditic (adj.): having both male and female reproductive parts.

hex: a spell cast to cause harm

inflorescence: several flowers closely grouped together to form one unit, or the particular arrangement of flowers on a plant

lobe: a rounded or projected part

lanceolate: shaped like a lance, tapering to a point at each end

leaflet: a small leaf or leaf-like part of a compound leaf

leguminous: an erect or climbing bean or pea plant

magick: metaphysical work to bring about change

mojo bag: a magic bag into which magickal items are placed and worn on the person

New Moon: the moon phase when the moon is not visible

oracle: a person who translates divination messages between people and the Other Worlds

ovate: egg-shaped with a broader end at the base

Pagan: originally meaning people who lived in the countryside and now meaning those who follow nature-based spirituality and hold beliefs other than the main religions of the world

perennial: a plant that lives for three or more years

pericarpel: the cup-like structure of a flower on which the petals or stamens sit

pinnate: feather-like

parasitic: gains all or part of its nutritional needs from another living plant

pseudanthium: a flower head consisting of many tiny flowers

raceme: inflorescence in which the main axis of the plant produces a series of flowers on lateral stalks

ray flower: a flower that resembles a petal

ritual: a ceremony that combines actions and sometimes words and music

sessile: attached without a stalk

stamen: the pollen-producing reproductive organ of a flower

staminal column: a structure, in column form, containing the male
reproductive organ of a plant

scrying: using a reflective surface or a body of water to gaze into during
divination

stem: the main part of a plant, usually rising above the ground

spent: flowers that have died

tepal: a segment in a flower that has no differentiation between petals and
sepals

thermogenic: the ability to generate and maintain heat

tuber: a thickened part of an underground stem

Vodoun: a religion created by African ethnic groups in colonial Saint-
Domingue and then blended with Christianity in the 16th and 17th
centuries

Waxing Moon: when the moon is getting larger, towards full

Waning Moon: when the moon is getting smaller, towards dark/new

Bibliography

Benzakein, Erin and Waite. Michele M., *Floret Farm's Cut Flower Garden*, (Chronicle Books 2007)

Byczynski, Lynn, *The Flower Farmer* (Chelsea Green Publishing 2008)

Clarke, Ian and Lee, Helen, *Name That Flower* (Melbourne University Press 1987)

Cook, Will, *Indoor Gardening* (TCK Publishing 2013)

Coombes, Allen J. *Dictionary of Plant Names* (Timber Press 2002)

Cunningham, Scott, *Encyclopedia of Magical Herbs* (Llewellyn Publications 2010)

Graves, Julia, *The Language of Plants* (Lindisfarne Books 2012)

Hanson, J. Wesley, *Flora's Dial* (Jonathan Allen 1846)

Harrison, Lorraine, *RHS Latin for Gardeners* (Mitchell Beazley 2012)

Hemphill, John & Rosemary, *Myths and Legends of the Garden* (Hodder & Stoughton 1997)

Hill, Lewis and Hill, Nancy, *The Flower Gardener's Bible* (Storey Publishing 2003)

Jay, Roni, *Sacred Flowers* (Thorsons 1997)

Kear, Katherine, *Flower Wisdom* (Beyond Words 2000)

Kelly, Frances, *Illustrated Language of Flowers* (Viking O'Neil 1992)

Macboy, Stirling *What Flower Is That?* (Lansdowne Press 2000)

Mac Coitir, Niall, *Irish Wild Plants* (Collins Press 2008)

Newbery, Georgie, *The Flower Farmer's Year* (UIT Cambridge Ltd 2015)

Olds, Margaret, *Flora's Plant Names* (Gordon Cheers 2003)

Pavord, Anna *The Naming of Names, The Search for Order in the World of Plants* (Bloomsbury 2005)

Phillips, Stuart, *An Encyclopaedia of Plants in Myth, Legend, Magic and Lore* (Robert Hale Limited 2012)

Potter, Jennifer, *Seven Flowers, and how they shaped our world* (Atlantic Books 2013)

Richardson, Fern, *Small-Space Container Gardens* (Timber Press 2012)

Sanders, Jack, *The Secrets of Wildflowers* (Lyons Press 2014)

Sulman, Florence, *A Popular Guide to Wild Flowers of New South Wales* (Angus & Robertson Ltd 1926)

Telesco, Patricia, *A Floral Grimoire* (Citadel Press 2001)

Vickery, Roy, *A Dictionary of Plant-Lore* (Oxford University Press 1995)

Ward, Bobby J. *A Contemplation Upon Flowers* (Timber Press 1999)

White, Ian, *Australian Bush Flower Healing* (Bantam Books 1999)

Image Credits

Page ii, Nesbit, E. *Spring (Summer-Autumn-Winter) songs and sketches* (Griffith, Farran and Co,London, 1886)

Page iv, Gilbert, Henry G. *Seed Annual 1898* (D.M. Ferry & Co, Detroit, Michigan, 1898)

Page v, F. R. Pierson Co Catalog Collection. *Choice Selections in Seeds and Plants* (F. R. Pierson Tarrytown, N. Y., 1892)

Page vii, Rose, A. M. *Armand de l'Isle* (Eden, Remington & Co. London 1893)

Page viii, Peters, Charles. *A Crown of Flowers* (Religious Tract Society, London 1883)

Page xi, Broughton, Rhoda. *Belinda. A Novel* (R. Bentley & Son, London, 1883)

Page xii, Mcgregor Bros. *1891 Floral Gems* (Henry G. Gilbert Nursery and Seed Catalog Collection 1891)

Page xvi, Hewlett, Maurice Henry. *A Masque of Dead Florentines* (J.M.Dent, London 1895)

Page ix, Dodge, Mary Mapes. *St. Nicholas* (Scribner & Co., New York, 1873)

Page xx, Valentini, M. B. *Newly Revised Garden of the Plant Kingdom* (1719)

FLOWER SPELLS FOR RELATIONSHIPS AND LOVE

Crane, Walter. *Flora's Feast* (Cassell & Co. London 1889)

Lisianthus and Red Rose New Love Spell

May, Philip. *Love: the Reward. A novel* (Remington & Co. London 1885)
Illustration: Prest, Thomas Peckett

Fuchsia and Agapanthus Rekindle Love Spell

Cobbe-Webbe, Christopher. *Haverfordwest and its Story* (Llewellyn Brigstocke, Haverfordwest 1882)

Peruvian Lily and Yellow Rose Friendship Spell

Rose, A. M. *Armand de l'Isle* (Eden, Remington & Co. London 1893)

Cosmos Communication Improvement Spell

Peters, Charles. *A Crown of Flowers* (Religious Tract Society, London 1883)

Red Tulip and Rosewater Passion Spell

Abbey, E. A. and Parsons, Alfred. *Old Songs* (Macmillan & Co. London 1889)

Hibiscus and Cyclamen Separation Spell

F.H. Horsford (Firm), *Horsford's Descriptive Catalogue* (Charlotte, Vt. 1894)

Golden Chrysanthemum Pet Protection Spell

Peter Henderson & Co's seed catalogue (Peter Henderson & Co. New York 1872)

Baby's Breath Flower Family Harmony Spell

Favourite flowers of garden and greenhouse. v.1 (London 1896)

Orchid Daily Self-Love Spell

Kirchhoff, Alfred. *Unser Wissen von der Erde* (Prag 1886)

Love-in-a-Mist Heart-Healer Spell

Valentini, M. B. *Newly Revised Garden of the Plant Kingdom* (1719)

FLOWER SPELLS FOR HAPPINESS AND HARMONY

Daisy Happiness Spell

Spring (Summer-Autumn-Winter) songs and sketches (Griffith, Farran and Co, London, 1886) Illustration: Nesbit, E. (Edith)

Poppy Painful Memory Healing Spell

Ritter, Pierre Henri - the Elder. *Eene halve Eeuw* (Amsterdam, 1898)

Daffodil Hope Renewal Spell

Robinson, Henry Peach *Pictorial Effect in Photography* (London, 1869)

White Lily and Rose Truth Spell

Fredensborg (Kjøbenhavn, 1896)

Frangipani Self-Confidence Spell

Norton, E.H., *Brazilian flowers* (1893)

Hyacinth Tension-Relief Spell

Maule, Henry (Firm) *The Maule Seed Book 1915* (Philadelphia, 1915)

Gerbera Daisy Blues Busting Spell

John Lewis Childs (Firm) *Childs' rare flowers, vegetables, and fruits* (Floral Park, N.Y. 1911)

Wild Rose and Geranium Stop Gossip Spell

McGregor Bros *Floral Gems* (Springfield, O.H. 1891)

Iris and Passion Flower Inspiration Spell

Broughton, Rhoda *Belinda. A Novel* (R. Bentley & Son, London, 1883)

Camellia and Freesia Calm Spell

Johnson & Stokes *1894 garden & farm manual* (Philadelphia, PA 1894)

FLOWER SPELLS FOR SUCCESS AND PROSPERITY

Crane, Walter. *A Flower Wedding* (Cassell & Company, London 1905)

Nasturtium Goal-Setting Spell

Reclus, Élisée. *The Earth and its Inhabitants* (London 1878) Illustration: Ravenstein, Ernst Georg

Delphinium Make-Things-Happen Spell

Iowa Seed Co. *26th Annual Catalogue* (Des Moines, Iowa, 1896)

African Violet Study and Exam Spell

Bailey, L.H. *Cyclopedia of American Horticulture* (Doubleday, Page & Company 1906)

Stargazer Lily Business Protection and Success Spell

Bailey, L.H. *Cyclopedia of American Horticulture* (Doubleday, Page & Company, 1906)

Carnation Decision Maker Spell

17th Annual Catalogue of the Germain Seed and Plant Co (Germain Seed and Plant Co, Los Angeles, Calif 1902)

Dandelion Wishing Spell

Andersen, H.C. *Stories for the Household* (G. Routledge and Sons, London, 1889)

Water Lily Psychic Ability Spell

Cobley, Frederick *On Foot through Wharfedale* (W. Walker & Sons, Otley, 1882)

Gladiolus Creativity Success Spell

Leonard, Anna B Robineau & Alsop, Adelaide Alsop. *Keramic Studio* (Keramic Studio Publishing Co, Syracuse, N.Y., 1865)

Scotch Thistle Flower Find-What-is-Lost Spell

Az Osztrák-Magyar Monarchia Austria (Budapest, 1885)

Yellow Rose New-Beginning Spell

Steckler's Seeds : 1905 (J. Steckler Seed Co, Steckler, New Orleans, La., 1905)

FLOWER SPELLS FOR PROTECTION AND CLEARING

Triple Rose Smudging Spell

Vick, James. *Vick's floral guide for 1875* (James Vick, Rochester, N.Y. 1875)

Snapdragon Hex-Breaker Spell

1912 Snapdragon Keramic Studio Magazine Illustration

Lilac Space-Clearing Spell

Whitney, Helen H. *Herbs and Apples Catalog* (New York 1910)

Sweet Violet Deception Protection Spell

Allen-Brown, A Allen-Brown, D. *The Violet Book* (J. Lane co., London, 1913)

Red Clover Travel Protection Spell

Division of Agrostology, United States *Bulletin* (Washington, D. C. 1895)

Azalea and Chrysanthemum Personal Protection Spell

McGregor Bros *1891 Floral Gems* (McGregor Bros., Springfield, O. H., 1891)

Cornflower Home Protection Spell

F. R. Pierson Co Catalog Collection *Choice Selections in Seeds and Plants* (F. R. Pierson Tarrytown, N. Y., 1892)

Lemon Blossom Freeze-and-Banish Spell

Orton, James. *The Andes and the Amazon* (Harper, New York 1876)

Heather Danger-Shielding Spell

Hertford, A. C. *Among the Heather* (Oliphant, Anderson & Co. Edinburgh and London, 1891)

Lavender Ultimate Protection Spell

Linné, Carl von. *Caroli a Linne* (Erlangae, sumtu J. J. Palm, 1785)

FLOWER SPELLS FOR HEALTH AND HEALING

Champion City Greenhouses *The Champion City Greenhouses* (Good & Reese Co., Springfield, Ohio, 1900)

Peony Vitality and Good Health Spell

Keble, John *The Christian Year* (London,1874)

Elderflower Rejuvenation Spell

Rogers, Julia Ellen *The tree book: A popular guide to a knowledge of the trees of North America and to their uses and cultivation* (Doubleday, New York, 1920)

Sunflower Strength and Courage Spell

The Artistic Language of Flowers. (G. Routledge & Sons, London, 1888)

Dahlia Detox Spell

Otto Schwill & Company *Catalogue 1918* (Memphis, Tenn., 1918)

Hibiscus Stress Release Spell

J.J.H. Gregory & Son *James J.H. Gregory & Son's catalogue of home grown seeds* (Marblehead, Mass. 1895)

Moonflower Stop Nightmares Spell

Otto Schwill & Company *1908 annual catalogue and price list: seeds of every description* (Memphis, Tenn. 1908)

Morning Glory Habit-Breaker Spell

Johnstone, David Lawson *The Brotherhood of the Coast* (W. & R. Chambers, London and Edinburgh, 1895)

White Chrysanthemum Health Commitment Spell

McGregor Bros *1891 Floral Gems* (Springfield, O. H., 1891)

Madonna Lily and Pink Rose Healing Spell

Peter Henderson & Co *Peter Henderson & Co.'s wholesale catalogue* (New York 1896)

Everlasting Daisy Immunity Spell

J. M. Philips' Sons. *1895 Seeds* (Mercersburg, Pa., 1895)

FLOWER SPELLS FOR TRANSITION AND CHANGE

Dodge, Mary Mapes. *St. Nicholas* (Scribner & Co., New York, 1873)

Gardenia Divination Spell

Fruitland Nurseries. *Fruit and ornamental trees, roses, etc* (Augusta, Ga., 1899)

Stephanotis Planning Spell

1892: bulbs, plants, seeds. For autumn planting. (Peter Henderson & Co, New York 1892)

Sacred Blue Water Lily Second-Chance Spell

Florists' Review 1912 (Florists' Pub. Co, Chicago 1912)

Sweet Alyssum Clarity Spell

WW Barnard & Co. *Seeds, bulbs, shrubs catalogue* (Chicago, Ill, 1914)

Magnolia New Home Search-and-Protect Spell

American Florists Company. *The American florist: a weekly journal for the trade* (Chicago, 1885)

Wild Rose New Beginning Spell
Meehan, Thomas. *The native flowers and ferns of the United States* (L. Prang and Co. Boston, 1898)

Tuberose Obstacle Remover Spell
Henry G. Gilbert Nursery and Seed Trade Catalog Collection. *Seed Annual 1898* (D.M. Ferry & Co, Detroit, Michigan, 1898)

Jasmine New Opportunity Spell
Miss Ella V. Baines, the woman florist, Springfield, Ohio: 1900 spring catalogue (Henry G. Gilbert Nursery, Springfield, Ohio, 1900)

Snowdrop Career and Last Change Spell
Barnard, Frederick, *Sunlight and Shade* (Cassell & Co. London, 1883)

Sweet-Pea Change Spell
Wm. Henry Maule (Firm), *1915 the Maule Seed Book* (Philadelphia, Pa., Maule 1915)

Hydrangea Problem Solving Spell
Liegeard, Stéphen. *La Côte d'Azur* (Paris, 1887)

HOW TO CREATE YOUR OWN SPELLS
Crane, Walter *A Floral Fantasy in an Old English Garden* (Harper & Bros, London, 1899)

FLOWER SPELL JOURNAL
Borders – *The Nobility of Life* Editor: Valentine, Laura, (London, 1869)

Acknowledgements

I would like to thank my mum, who spent many hours sharing her wisdom and laughter, keeping alive our family magick while I created this book.

Thanks to Pip, my dear friend, who has a magickal gift for making things a little better and brighter for everyone. Your assistance and support are invaluable to me. Jan, what can I say? Nothing. You would probably correct me anyway, but I love you for it. So thank you for listening to me while I wrote this book.

My crazy family, I probably make you that way while I research, grow stuff, make things and test it on you all and constantly fill conversations with botanical myths, history and mayhem. I appreciate you all and love you to Kazinus and back again. And you are right – it probably would be good to eat a salad occasionally without a botanical history lesson. But would it be as fun? I think not.

To the beautiful Blossoms who read my titles, own them and chat with me on social media; who come along to the libraries, stores, gardens and shows and send me very lovely emails. Thank you for sharing your passion for gardening, botanical wonderment and friendship with me. You fill my days with smiles, which I treasure and which keep me writing.

Everyone at Rockpool Publishing, again thank you for supporting my work with flowers, gardening and botanical history. Thanks for believing in Nature and in the need to share lost wisdoms with the world.

And last but most importantly, I would like to thank my precious garden. Thank you for the lessons and the joy. I could not write one word about flowers and their plants without you. But you know that, don't you. Thanks for sharing the magick with me. I love you.

About the author

heralyn Darcey is a botanical explorer, organic gardener, independent natural history scholar, artist, educator and the author of several books and oracle decks of nature magick, folklore, witchcraft and ethnobotanical traditions. Inspired by her pagan family upbringing and her passion for nature and magick, her work focuses on the spiritual, cultural, therapeutic and physical connections between humans and plants.

Her publications include three flower-reading oracle decks which bring the Language of Flowers through the Doctrine of Signatures alive: *The Australian Wildflower Reading Cards, Flower Reading Cards, Flowers of the Night Oracle*. A flower affirmation deck for daily guidance: *Flower Petals*. Two Australian Wildflower mandala style colouring books: *Florasphere Calm* and *Florasphere Inspire*. Her book *Flowerpaedia, 1,000 flowers and their meanings* presents a language translator for the Language of Flowers complete with correspondence lists to find flowers to match sentiments, ritual use and occasions.

For more information, visit www.cheralyndarcey.com

The Book of Herb Spells

ISBN 978-1-925682-26-7

Herbs can heal, comfort and nourish us with ancient energies used throughout time to create magickal spells.

Includes:

- Sixty sacred herb spells
- Spellcasting and spellcrafting basics
- Magickal gardening
- Dedicated lessons on how to write and cast your own spells
- A personal grimoire journal section

Explore magickal power with everyday sacred herbs!

Available from all good bookstores or online.